I0605332

Pimento Cheese

Other books by Rebecca Lang

Southern Entertaining for a New Generation

Mary Mac's Tea Room

Quick-Fix Southern

Around the Southern Table

Fried Chicken

The Southern Vegetable Book

Pecans

Y'all Come Over

Pimento Cheese

The Southern Spread

Rebecca Lang

Photography by Kathryn McCrary

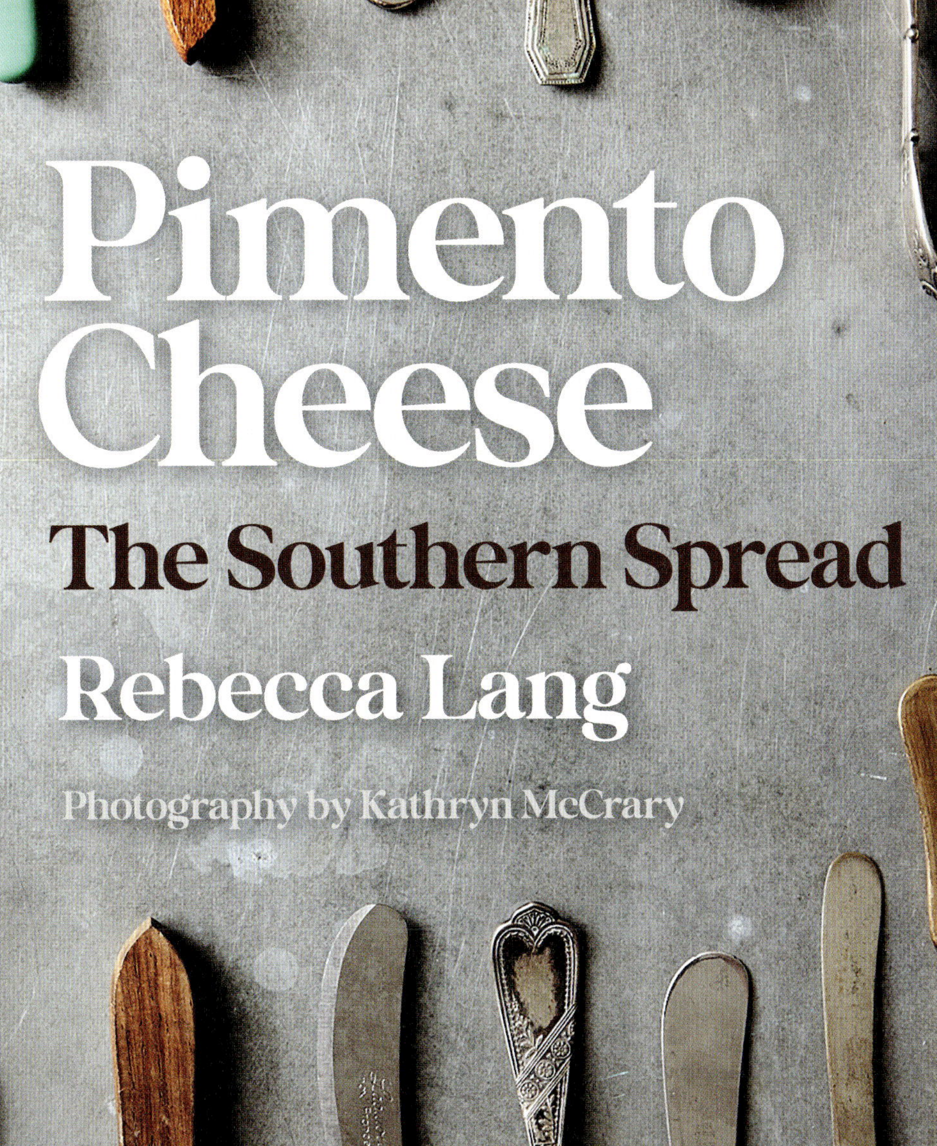

The University of Georgia Press ⌒ Athens

Publication of this work was made possible, in part, by support from the University of Georgia Press Friends Fund

Published by the University of Georgia Press
Athens, Georgia 30602
www.ugapress.org

Designed by Erin Kirk
Set in Miller Text
Printed and bound by Versa Press
The paper in this book meets the guidelines for permanence and durability of the Committee on Production Guidelines for Book Longevity of the Council on Library Resources.

Printed in the United States of America
30 29 28 27 26 c 5 4 3 2

EU Authorized Representative
Easy Access System Europe—Mustamäe tee 50, 10621 Tallinn, Estonia, gpsr.requests@easproject.com

Library of Congress Control Number: 2025035317
ISBN: 9780820374673

For Mimi and Papa,
the most enthusiastic pimento cheese
tasters I know

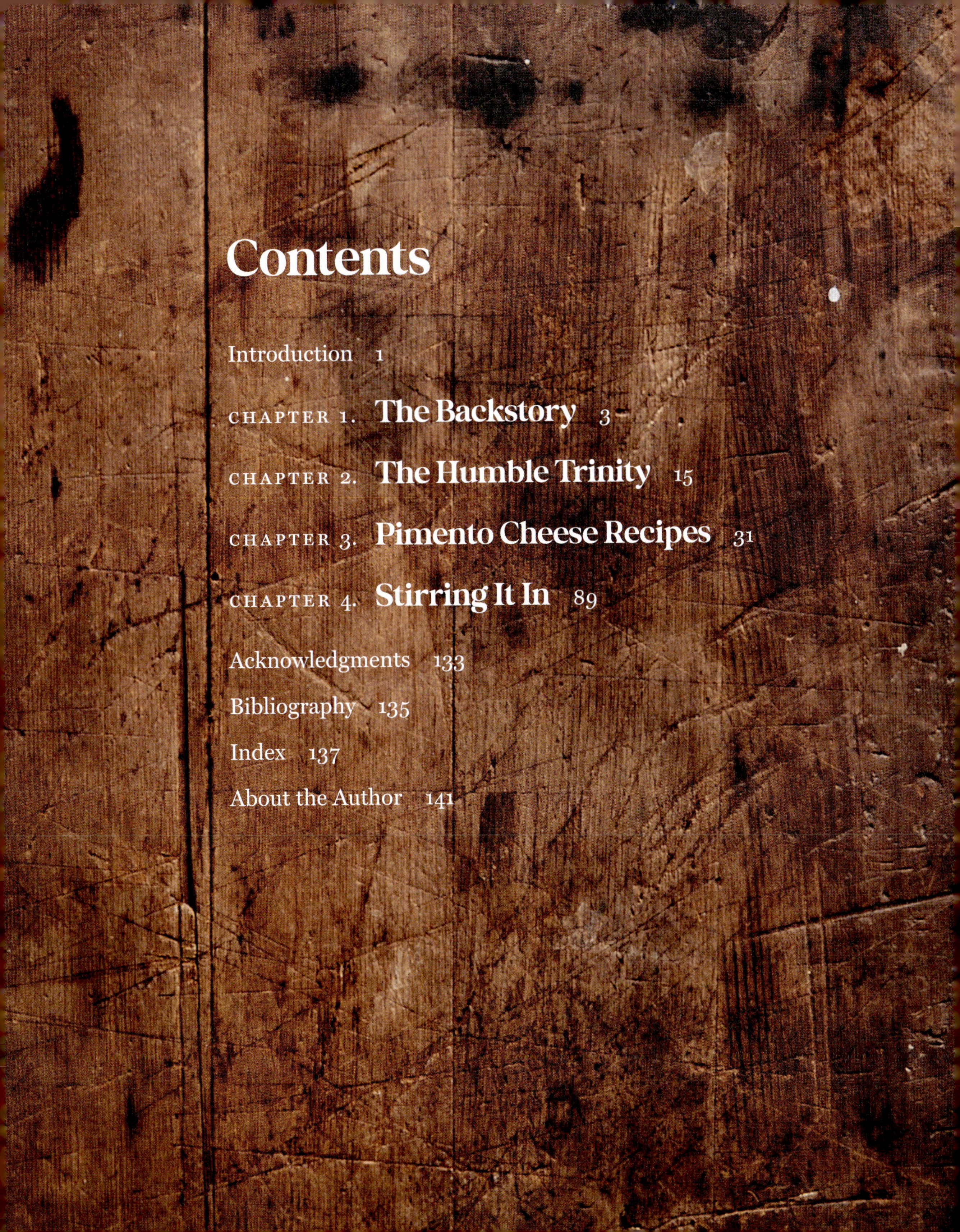

Contents

KUM
UNI
MADE IN GERMANY

Pimento Cheese

Coca-Cola
ORIGINAL TASTE

Introduction

Unlike almost all foods, pimento cheese knows no boundaries of class, income, or address. Pimento cheese sandwiches were sold by women on "dope carts" to workers in textile mills. They are served to the best golfers in the world at the finest of golf tournaments. They are still a working-class food to take to factories in order to eat quickly and return to the production line. To this day, you can find 1½-pound tubs of it at Walmart for less than seven dollars and on menus of upscale restaurants in Los Angeles and New York. Pimento cheese is served at country church funeral receptions in Lumber City, Georgia, and on expensive, crustless white bread for tea at the Ritz-Carlton in Atlanta. It is truly a food of the South that belongs to us all.

I don't recall a time in my life that we didn't have pimento cheese. Thinking back to so many events that really mattered, pimento cheese was on the menu. I've thought and thought and tried my best to remember my first experience with the famous Southern spread. It's like air and water. It's always been there.

For eleven years during my childhood, the first day of summer break also meant the start to our local swim team practices. The McRae Minnows were the highlight of the season. I'm sure my parents thought differently as they sweated at swim meets for hours waiting for our races on what had to feel like the face of the sun. In a town as small as my hometown, everything was within a bicycle ride's distance, including my elementary school, the pool, and the apartment my grandmother Tom lived in. Her front porch faced the pool that was practically a part-time home for me during swim season. As if I never learned that hot asphalt and feet don't mix, I would teeter across the road barefoot to her door, slightly wrapped in a towel, squeaking because the pavement was so hot. I might find a snack of fatback, sugar cookies with the imprint of fork tines in the top, or pimento cheese. All of the above came with a

Coke. When the cracks in the street were tarred to give a few more years of life to the local road, I thought it was so fun to stick my toes in the black squishy lines. I was obviously easily occupied.

Tom sat on the front porch much of the time, and the hoopla from swim practice must have given her some entertainment. She rocked there on warm summer days with a block of sharp cheddar cheese and her favorite glass bowl nearly etched from all the love it had seen in her kitchen. With sunshine and strong, nearly hundred-year-old fingers that had worked way more than their fair share over a lifetime, she crumbled the cheese to the consistency of small curds. No tools or fancy gadgets were needed, just heat and the best kitchen tools that God gave us all—our hands. It was the way she learned from her mother. Once inside, she added real mayonnaise and pimentos, and a glorious union was created for those of us lucky enough to have a taste. Combined with the softest white bread in the world and a real bottle of Coca-Cola, it made life instantly fine. Tom was a master at pimento cheese and never needed a recipe, a cookbook, or a cooking show to inspire her to such an outcome.

I've now made more batches of pimento cheese than most people will in a lifetime. Some are spicy, some are sweet, some tangy, with textures that vary from spreadable to chunky. But it's still Tom's that I favor more than any other. A food like pimento cheese doesn't earn lifelong cravings with ingredients and flavor alone. It's often the love of the cook that first made it that's indelibly tied to the recipe.

Chapter 1
The Backstory

It's hard to imagine a Southern picnic, tailgate, or bridal shower without pimento cheese. The connection we hold to the sacred spread is real and nearly spiritual. We owe the state of New York the world's largest thank-you note for bringing it into our lives. The original pimento cheese looked quite different from what we make today. I've known Southern women who will sit and debate the rights and wrongs of adding cream cheese to pimento cheese. Many will be dismayed that the original combination was only cream cheese and pimentos.

The first cream cheese in America was made in the 1870s in Chester, New York, by one William Lawrence, who aimed to make a creamier version of Neufchâtel. Peppers from Spain began to be imported into America as cream cheese was being perfected in New York. As the peppers grew in popularity, they were sold under their Spanish name, pimientos. It took only about ten years for that second *i* to be dropped and the shortened spelling "pimento" to appear in most mentions. Magazines were already featuring recipes with cream cheese and pimentos.

Store shelves began to carry cream cheese already studded with bright red pimentos, ready to spread in order to make meal preparation easier. By the spring of 1910, grocery stores in Minnesota were advertising "Pimento Cheese—Something New." This new pimento cheese was a home economist's dream, and its popularity grew across the country.

Pimentos were growing in California from Spanish seeds thought to have been obtained through the United States Department of Agriculture. Southern California was hot and dry, and the peppers thrived. In a way, the seeds from Spain were just returning to their home continent. Christopher Columbus took seeds from the New World back to Spain on his second voyage. It's one of the ways he proved he had found the "spicy islands." The peppers became a profitable crop in Spain.

As pimentos were flourishing on the West Coast to an estimated annual worth of $500,000 in the early 1910s, a pimento explosion on the East Coast was beginning. In less than twenty years, Georgia was the largest grower and canner of pimentos. The U.S. Labor Department credits the low pay in the South with the toppling of the pimento in California. Georgia's cannery workers, mostly women, earned twenty cents an hour, about half of the hourly pay in the Golden State. By the 1950s, Georgia was growing more than 90 percent of pimentos in the United States.

By the late 1920s, pimento cheese was the answer to lunch for workers in mills in the Carolinas that didn't have an official lunch break. Pimento cheese sandwiches were economical and portable. Small food manufacturers began to make pimento cheese to fill the need of mill commissaries and small restaurants that fed workers for a quick midday meal. But as mills closed and the textile industry moved overseas, those food manufacturers slowly closed as well. Only a few survived the economic blow. Ruth's, in Charlotte, North Carolina, began in 1953 as a small community pimento cheese company and is now the largest producer of commercial pimento cheese. The brown bag lunch is still alive, especially in areas with a higher population working in manufacturing. In these areas, Ruth's sales are booming.

Pimento cheese was touted in magazines and newspapers as a packaged ingredient, not as a recipe to make. After World War II, pimento cheese was increasingly made at home as opposed to being just another item on the grocery list. The transition from cream cheese and pimentos to hoop cheese and pimentos is a historically fuzzy one. Perhaps because of the huge economic impact that pimentos had on Georgians, it was Southerners who first used cheeses like hoop cheese to replace the North's cream cheese. Some believe that making a homemade version using hoop cheese was simply less expensive than buying the prepacked cream-cheese-based spread. Hoop cheese was produced in country stores, and it was economical. But with a grated semi-firm cheese like hoop or cheddar, something creamy was needed to hold the ingredients together. Mayonnaise was a staple in almost every household and became the binder of choice. The pimento cheese we know today was forged in Southern kitchens by women who likely wanted to re-create a marketing masterpiece with ingredients that they could afford and that they already had on hand.

The Pimento State

In 1888 the Georgia state legislature charged that a center be dedicated to agricultural research, complete with scientists to tackle the dilemmas faced by the state's farmers. Educating farmers on countless issues, including soil health and pest control, became an important aspect of the newly formed Georgia Experiment Station, near Griffin.

This farmer education was the birth of agricultural extension programs in the state. Seed development attempted to overcome disasters like the boll weevil. While the Experiment Station worked to keep the cotton industry alive, its scientists planned to make sure Georgia had a backup crop to the famed peach that could match the fuzzy fruit's popularity and economic impact. That insurance policy was the pimento.

Georgia agricultural experts who saw a need for domestically grown pimentos got to work near Griffin. A historical marker still stands at the Georgia Experiment Station for pioneering work in developing many crops, including the Truhart pimento.

S. D. Riegel and Sons from Experiment, Georgia, released the Truhart pimento in 1912. As the Riegel family tried different seeds in hopes of perfecting the pimento in Georgia soil, they realized seeds from Spain would be necessary to achieve the level of quality they desired. They were indeed able to procure pimento seeds from Spain, thanks to their congressman, Charles L. Bartlett. With those seeds the Riegels worked to improve the pepper, using mostly selective breeding. The Perfection and Truhart Perfection pimento varieties were born. The Riegels founded the canning business named Pomona Products Company in Griffin. They also invented a machine that roasted the peppers and made peeling the thick pimento skin exponentially quicker and easier. The canning plant was so successful that it wasn't long before other plants were up and running in other Georgia towns like Wayside, Bradley, Vienna, Macon, Meansville, Jackson, and Woodbury. Eventually, more than twenty canning plants called Georgia home.

At its most productive, Pomona Products Company alone was producing ten million cans of pimentos a year. The stars were aligning for pimento cheese to rise as a household staple. As a plethora of pimentos were grown in the state, and cheese was becoming more available in stores, commodity cheese became a part of life for many families. Color food photography was appearing in national magazines, and pimentos were noticed for their bright color and vivid garnishing ability. Georgia pimento sales rose to eventually overtake the monopoly on the market held by Spain. Georgia's peak production was from the mid-1920s to around 1950. Georgia pimentos were shipped to all corners of the United States. Kraft Foods Company was procuring its pimentos from Georgia. By 1950, shipments of Georgia pimentos were exported to Canada and the Philippines.

The father of the head of the Department of Horticulture at the University of Georgia returned home from a trip to Cuba in 1891 with several cans of Spanish pimentos. These are thought to be the first pimentos ever to enter Georgia.

Pimento packing season was from August 1 to November 15. To avoid closing down the plants when the season ended, canners found other foods to can and make sure the equipment was not sitting idle for the other three-quarters of the year. Citrus, field peas, peanut butter, snap beans, dates, and more were all added to schedules at canneries around the state. Even Brunswick stew was canned and helped to provide jobs year-round.

Woodbury, Georgia, became the Pimento Capital of the World. Like other small towns with an agricultural claim to fame, Woodbury held a yearly pageant to crown the reigning queen of the prized crop. Georgia's Cordele has the Watermelon Queen, Vidalia hosts the coronation of Miss Vidalia Onion, and Alma crowns a yearly Miss Georgia Blueberry. Bettye Jean Waddell was named the very first Pimento Queen in Woodbury in 1950. Her father was, of course, a pimento farmer.

Although once home to more than 32,000 acres of pimentos during the peak years, Georgia grows very little of the mighty pepper today. Disease, insects, and the intensity of labor slowly got the best of the crop. However, the pimento made its mark on Georgia's economy. The little pepper created thousands of jobs. Most important, through the processing plants' innovations, the industry of canning was improved for generations to come.

Pimento Cheese Sandwiches and Women

Even before women could vote in America, making and selling pimento cheese sandwiches began to provide an outlet to work from home and help support their families. Selling sandwiches in the mills on a dope cart (the carts also sold Coca-Cola, known then by the slang term "dope") was profitable in a time with little options for females wanting to bring in extra earnings. Eugenia Duke is the best-known example from that time. Duke sold sandwiches with her now famous mayonnaise and pimento cheese at Fort Sevier, near her home in Greenville, South Carolina. The canteens, run by the YMCA, were her first step in a very prosperous life in business.

In 1928, Karlie Keith Fisher started a business in the basement kitchen of her Raleigh, North Carolina, home, making pimento cheese sandwiches and snacks. Fisher later opened a restaurant in order to expand. She sold candy in addition to her sweets and sandwiches and eventually became one of the largest candy distributors in the Southeast.

Ruth Ross and her husband founded Ruth's (still in business today) in the early 1950s in Charlotte, North Carolina. The base for the business was Ruth's homemade pimento cheese, sold commercially with a marketing slogan of "Less Work for Mother."

The Tournament

Press coverage of the Masters is often credited with fanning the flames of the obsession with pimento cheese. During that very special week in April each year, it's not hard to find a golf reporter on television holding a microphone in one hand and a green-wrapped sandwich in the other. The sandwiches, even now, are only $1.50 and are made of gloriously soft white bread slathered with the most debated pimento cheese in the world.

The mystique of the course at the Augusta National Golf Club carries all the way to each and every perfectly manicured blade of grass. The azaleas bloom as if on cue from the heavens, no tree limbs or pinecones lie on the ground even after morning storms, and the food is fresh, costs almost nothing, and is sold in the neatest and most orderly concession stands on the planet.

The Beginning

Pimento cheese has a long history at the Masters but it often leaves out the origins of the unpretentious sandwich that is practically embedded in the world's most famous golf tournament. It's rare to read about Ola and Hodges Herndon and how their small home kitchen was the birthplace of pimento cheese at the Masters. In 1947 the Herndons began what would forever set the tone for expectations of golf concessions and countless conversations about pimento cheese. It is their nearly lost legacy that egg salad and pimento cheese are now practically synonymous with golf in Augusta, Georgia.

Their story is not filled with the glitz and glamour that tales of the Augusta National often include. Mr. Hodges Herndon owned a small restaurant and managed food service at the local VA hospital in Augusta. After being interviewed by Clifford Roberts, the cofounder of the Masters, Herndon was tasked with making sandwiches for the golf patrons at a price of twenty-five cents. The Herndons' two-bedroom, one-bathroom home became a temporary production kitchen for one week a year. The purchase of extra-large mixing bowls and a meat slicer aided the couple in cranking out the pimento cheese, egg salad, and ham sandwiches before delivering them to the course five miles away. Even Mrs. Herndon's friends joined in to help with the sandwich making. A kitchen full of ladies hopefully provided some lightheartedness and laughs to the impressive operation.

In the seventy-seven years since Mr. and Mrs. Herndon worked so hard to provide the famous sandwiches, the price has increased by only $1.25.

Like most Southern women who made pimento cheese then, Ola didn't have a recipe that she followed. It was simply a combination of a few good, modest ingredients that she turned into something amazing. The number of patrons grew, and the Herndons kept the sandwiches coming. Their son Tom helped by delivering the sandwiches up Berckmans Road several times a day. The exact number of pickup-truck loads of sandwiches that entered the gates to the course is unknown, but it had to have been a tremendous amount. Tom even had his Phi Delta Theta fraternity brothers from the University of Georgia join in. Of course, skipping class to be in Augusta all week needed permission. Fortunately, the boys were enrolled in the business school, and as long as they kept their grades up, their professor would allow them time off for some real-life business experience.

The Herndon grandchildren have a letter written to their grandparents in 1948 by Bobby Jones and Clifford Roberts, cofounders of Augusta National. The "good service and food" were praised by the two legends of the game of golf. Their respect for Hodges Herndon was also reflected in what is now one of the rarest Masters keepsakes in existence. The 1948 gift to tournament players was a solid brass ashtray featuring the thirteenth hole of the Augusta National Golf Club. Mr. Herndon received a personalized ashtray, the same as the fifty-seven players.

The Herndon granddaughters, Virginia Herndon Stutsman and Eleanor Herndon VanLandingham, and great-grandchildren still attend the Masters each year and partake in sandwiches just like other patrons. But they know that each bite is a direct result of the overwhelming hard work from their family so many years ago. Only the Herndons' descendants have a direct connection to the beginning of what is now the pinnacle of tournament concessions, beloved far beyond Augusta National.

The Age of Rangos

Caterer Nick Rangos took the helm at the Masters and filled the pimento cheese need for nearly fifty years. Rangos operated the Woodruff Drugs Soda Fountain down the road from Augusta (and across the state line) in Aiken, South Carolina. He was known to have the best pimento cheese recipe around, and word must have reached the powers that be at the Augusta National. Renowned golfer Ben Hogan even raved about Rangos's pimento cheese to other golfers and instructed them to head to the concession stand right away and "get yourself a good pimento cheese. Because you'll never have any better." Like the Herndons' son, the Rangos children would chip in. They became carriers of five-gallon tubs of the South's favorite spread. Their perk was getting to sit in the parked car above the first fairway and watch the golfers start their rounds.

The Drama

In 1998 the National removed the contract for pimento cheese from Rangos and passed it to WifeSaver restaurant franchise owner Ted Godfrey. The change of command did not set well with Rangos. Understandably, he declined to pass on his recipe to the Masters or to Godfrey. That meant Godfrey and the WifeSaver team had a lot of work to do to re-create the recipe. For such a simple concoction, it proved nearly impossible to nail down exactly what was missing. A frozen batch of the original was found and, remarkably, Godfrey was able to reverse-engineer the recipe to finally master a near replica of Rangos's recipe. For nearly fifteen years the pimento cheese drama lay dormant.

Then in 2013 concessions for the Masters all went in-house, and local supplier contracts were terminated. History repeated itself, and the pimento cheese recipe was held tight by its owner. PimentoGate was born. Patrons noticed the change. Reporters were bewildered by the difference. ESPN even investigated. As the scandal died down, the recipe was ironed out in succeeding years to keep patrons happy and unbothered. In Georgia, when the topic of pimento cheese and golf comes up, it's not unusual to hear a whisper of "Do you remember when the recipe changed?" And everyone always does.

Pimento Cheese Without Limits

I've been eating pimento cheese as long as I can remember. Certainly I have been making it for over forty years, professionally and nonprofessionally. My fondest childhood memories were never without this creamy, pungent Southern spread. Whether I indulged in pimento cheese on a buttery Ritz cracker, piped into the canal of a crisp celery rib, or tucked between the halves of a hot little biscuit, I have learned over the years that there are no limits to my love affair with pimento cheese. Snacking on pimento cheese is how it all began, but now I find myself incorporating it into meals, all of the above, morning, noon, and night.

It seems that pimento cheese is one of the South's best assets, but luckily for the rest of the country, others are now seeing its value and dolloping with much delight. There is just something so comforting, satisfying, and nostalgic about this delicious dip! At the end of the day, it's the memories that take me back to my grandmama's fridge on a hot day at the lake in the mountains that will forever seal my affinity to the greatest Southern staple!

Carrie Morey

Owner, Callie's Hot Little Biscuit
Charleston, South Carolina

Chapter 2
The Humble Trinity

sharp cheddar
extra sharp white cheddar
medium cheddar
sharp white cheddar
mild cheddar
extra sharp cheddar

It's not often that an entire region falls in love with a food. With only three very common ingredients stirred together to create one of the most beloved mixtures of all time, it's important to get to know cheese, pimentos, and mayonnaise.

Cheese

Cheddar 101

You'll find recipes in the coming pages highlighting other cheeses that work beautifully with pimentos. But for the most part, cheddar has replaced hoop cheese as the star in the South for pimento cheese recipes. We often take this common cheese for granted and fail to place it on a pedestal with fancier, more sophisticated cheeses. Cheddar is actually named for a village in Somersetshire, England, where the cheddar we now know originated. Cheddar is naturally a white cheese, but to achieve the bright orange that Americans expect, the spice annatto is added. Know what you're buying and what the descriptions mean. There are four designations of cheddar ripening. The longer the cheddar is aged, the sharper the flavor will be.

Mild cheddar is aged two to four months.
Medium cheddar is aged four to eight months.
Sharp cheddar is aged nine to twelve months.
Extra-sharp cheddar is aged more than one year.

The history of hoop cheese is largely linked to country stores dotted across the South. The cheeses could vary greatly in texture and sharpness, as each store would follow its own recipe using local cow's milk. The cheesemaking took place frequently, as no preservatives were used, so the shelf life was short. When real cheese hoops weren't available for shaping the cheese, farmers and storekeepers were known to make do with wooden hoop-shaped molds of any kind. The wheels of cheese were often coated in red or black wax to help with preservation. As country stores disappeared from the rural landscape in the mid-1900s, so did the highly prized small-batch hoop cheese. Mass-produced hoop cheese can be found in grocery stores now, but it's a closer relative to Cheddar and Monterey Jack than the cherished and unique versions from years ago.

Shredding

Although buying pre-shredded cheese is tempting if you're in a hurry, I always prefer shredding my own cheese. An eight-ounce block of cheddar will yield two cups of shredded cheese. It's almost always less expensive to purchase a block of cheese than to purchase pre-shredded.

If you know you'll need a lot of shredded cheese in the next week, shred away! There's no need to reinvent the shred for each recipe. I like to shred, measure, put in an airtight container, label, and refrigerate. A good general rule to remember is: The softer your cheese, the colder it should be for shredding. Never will a room-temperature cheese be best for shredding by hand. I've often thrown cheese, even cheddar, in the freezer for a few minutes before shredding. It always helps.

Why Grate Your Own?

When you buy pre-shredded cheese, you are buying much more than cheese. Take a close look inside the bag, and you'll see that each shred of cheese has the faintest powdery look. Preservatives are added to keep the cheese from clumping, most commonly powdered cellulose (derived from wood pulp), potato starch, and natamycin. Because these additives keep the shreds from clumping, they hinder the cheese from melting properly and having the desired creamy mouthfeel that freshly shredded blocks of cheese can offer.

So not only is pre-shredded almost always more expensive, the convenience does not outweigh the subpar quality.

Measuring

Cheese weight can vary depending on its softness, even when measured in the same measuring cup.

The softer the cheese, the heavier the weight. For example, one cup of blue cheese weighs six ounces, while one cup of cheddar cheese weights four ounces.

How to Store

It's a general rule that the harder the cheese, the longer it can be stored. Softer cheeses, like goat cheese, are best refrigerated for no more than two weeks after opening, as the quality then degrades quickly. Before opening, cheddar and harder cheeses like Parmesan can be refrigerated for four months, but once the package is opened, they should be used within three weeks.

Keep all cheeses in the vegetable crisper drawer or, if you're lucky, the cheese drawer. This will keep them the coldest, with a regulated humidity. Take a peek through the fridge. Remove any items that are moldy. Those spores can release and have a negative effect on your cheese.

For hard, aged cheeses like Parmigiano-Reggiano, I like to wrap them in parchment paper and then put them in a plastic bag. Blues are best put in a plastic bag with just a touch of air left in. Cheddar and gouda should be wrapped tightly in cheese paper or waxed paper.

If cheese is packed in a tub of water, like mozzarella or feta, keep it in the original packaging and try to remember to change the water every few days.

Essential Equipment

I've spent more time with box graters than any person should. You have to pay attention not to grate yourself too, but otherwise they are really smart, simple pieces of equipment. Two inventors, one English, one French, both claimed to have invented the first cheese grater in the mid-1500s. But as the need for grated cheese eventually reached North America, shapes of graters varied tremendously. Some were dials, some had knuckle protectors, some were half cylinders, and others were folded models with varying hole sizes. American frontier entrepreneur Jacob Bromwell invented the box grater in the early 1800s.

Food Processor vs. Box Grater

There is a difference in the texture of cheeses when grated in a food processor rather than on a box grater. Food processor blades tend to produce more of a rounded shred, while box graters give a flatter slice. Shreds from a food processor will be not only more circular but usually longer. In most cases that doesn't matter, but it's good to know. If I have more than a pound of cheese to grate, I use the food processor every time. It's harder to clean but well worth the time saved.

A box grater has four sides, each for a different purpose. One side does slicing; one may have spiky protrusions that can zest a lemon or grate a nutmeg; the other two or three have uniform holes of distinct sizes. The large holes are most commonly used for cheese grating. Try using them also for potatoes and for very cold butter. The fine holes work well for garlic and fresh ginger.

microplane
box grater
large holes
box grater
medium holes

Pimentos

Pimentos 101

Pimentos are a sweet Spanish pepper ranking as one of the lowest on the Scoville heat scale. When fresh, they look like a slightly smaller bright red bell pepper that's trying to grow into a heart shape. Pimentos top out at about an inch and a half across. They are especially thick-skinned, with meatier flesh than a bell pepper. Because of this, they are at their best when peeled and processed.

It's much more common to see jars of the treasured pepper than to ever find a fresh pimento in the grocery store. Long before pimentos found their perfect match in cheese, they were cherished for their ability to balance out the saltiness of olives with some sweetness. The technique of stuffing the center of pitted olives with pimentos is thought to date back as far as the 1700s in France.

Spanish paprika is smoked, as opposed to the Hungarian-style sweet paprika commonly sold in America, and is known as pimentón. It is not made from pimentos.

Pimiento vs. Pimento

Read enough pimento cheese recipes and you'll be a bit confused about the spelling of the peppers at the center of the obsession. "Pimento" and "pimiento" are both correct. "Pimiento," the original Spanish spelling (also the generic term for all peppers), was shortened in English to "pimento" over time. I prefer "pimento" since it's what I grew up recognizing as the world's most important pepper.

Shopping and Storing

Jarred pimentos are readily available and can be purchased diced, sliced, and whole. Most diced and sliced pimentos come in jar sizes of 2 ounces, 4 ounces, and 7 ounces. The 2-ounce jars are still available but can be harder to find. Once opened, pimento jars should be stored in the refrigerator. Pimentos mold fairly quickly and should be used within a week of opening.

Until the late 1880s, "pimento" and "allspice" were interchangeable terms for the dried unripe berries of the *Pimenta dioica*, a plant native to the West Indies, southern Mexico, and Central America. Also called Jamaica pepper, allspice is so named because its flavor evokes a mix of other spices.

To Drain or Not to Drain?

Make sure to follow the individual recipe on directions for draining. Some recipes need the brine that the peppers are packed in for extra moisture. Some require draining and even patting dry as an added step to remove all excess water. When I pat dry, I lay a few layers of paper towel on a plate, add the drained pimentos, and then pat with more paper towels until liquid stops being absorbed.

Substitutions

Using roasted red bell peppers in pimento cheese, rather than the smaller cut pimentos, is done very often and is a fun way to have larger pieces of peppers in recipes. I like the jarred versions that still have some of the char on the peppers. Or make your own roasted bell peppers.

Just in case you have a larger or smaller jar size than the recipe calls for:

- **2-ounce jar of drained diced pimentos = 3 tablespoons pimentos**
- **4-ounce jar of drained diced pimentos = 6 tablespoons pimentos**
- **7-ounce jar of drained diced pimentos = 10 tablespoons pimentos**

Diced Pimiento
95%

Roasting Your Own Peppers

Preheat the broiler. Cut red or orange bell peppers in half lengthwise; discard the seeds and membranes. Place the halves, skin side up, on a foil-lined sheet pan and flatten them with your hand. Broil for eight minutes or until totally blackened. Wrap the bell peppers in foil and let stand for ten minutes. Remove and discard the blackened skins. Roasted and peeled peppers can be stored in an airtight container in the refrigerator for four days.

So.Many.Jars

I never throw away a pimento jar. The more pimento cheese you make, the more jars you'll save. Get creative and reuse! I love turning them into little bud vases and tea-light holders and match jars for giving away. Just order self-adhesive match strike paper online and fill with your favorite matches for a thoughtful hostess gift. My grandmother was a florist and liked to put copper pennies in the bottom of vases with tulips. The copper kept the stems upright. I keep old pennies that were still made of mostly copper in a pimento jar. In the kitchen, I store salt and pepper in pimento jars and also use them for making vinaigrette dressings.

Mayonnaise

Mayonnaise 101

Most Southern cooks will tell you that there's no finer and more versatile ingredient than mayonnaise. It makes just about everything better. It's known for pimento cheese, deviled eggs, chicken salad, and tomato sandwiches. A chocolate cake with mayonnaise in the batter is moist and rich beyond compare. Mashed potatoes made with mayonnaise are simply dreamy. A dollop of mayonnaise tucked into the hollow of a canned pear half has been served by Southern grandmothers nearly forever. Slathering it onto the outer sides of bread before making a grilled cheese sandwich is a game changer. Even cake mix and pancake batter benefit from a little mayonnaise.

It can take just a few minutes of conversation to lead into a passionate debate about which brand is the very best. On any given day, you will only find Duke's mayonnaise in my kitchen. I think the texture is creamier, it has no sugar to sweeten it up, and it's more tangy than other brands. Even when other brands are buy-one-get-one-free and I'm tempted for a moment at the grocery store, I always come back to my senses before checking out. But I'm like a lot of fortysomethings in the South. I didn't know Duke's when I was growing up. I was raised on Hellmann's and didn't think a thing about it. My parents' house is one that is divided. My mom has come over to my side and buys Duke's for her beloved summer tomato sandwiches. My dad is fiercely loyal to Hellmann's. I guess it works. They've been married fifty-five years.

Duke's

Duke's mayonnaise has a history deeply rooted in the South and a legendary following of cooks that are religious about using it and nothing else. Eugenia Duke started her mayonnaise empire by making chicken salad, pimento cheese, and egg salad sandwiches using her homemade mayonnaise and selling them to soldiers at Fort Sevier near Greenville, South Carolina, in 1917. Soldiers were training for World War I, and Mrs. Duke saw an opportunity. Sandwiches were ten cents each. During the war, sugar was scarce, so it was left out of her mayonnaise recipe. That made all the difference. It took Mrs. Duke one year and eleven thousand sandwiches to purchase her first delivery truck. After selling sandwiches in grocery stores and other locations, she stopped producing sandwiches and began to bottle her mayonnaise in 1923 in Greenville. She sold the company in 1929, yet the recipe remains the same to this day.

Staying True to the South

Depending on where your mail is delivered, other Southern mayonnaise brands may be the star of your pimento cheese. Blue Plate mayonnaise was first made in Louisiana in the late 1920s. It's prized for its rich flavor and creamy texture, thanks to being made with only egg yolks. Cajun chefs sing its praises as their hometown prized product. Blue Plate was made in an iconic building that became a landmark in New Orleans. Blue Plate was bought by Reily Foods Company in 1974, and the original factory is on the National Register of Historic Places.

JFG Real Mayonnaise was first produced in 1919 by JFG wholesale grocer in Knoxville. Known and beloved, thanks to being made with apple cider vinegar, it's now also owned by Reily Foods. Both Blue Plate and JFG are made in Knoxville.

The moral of the mayonnaise story is to have some fun and make some pimento cheese with several different mayonnaises. It's the most delicious and responsible way to choose which brand deserves your loyalty.

Making Your Own Mayonnaise

When store-bought mayonnaise is as good as Duke's, it's hard to feel the need to make your own. But it's true that homemade mayonnaise is one of the finest things to taste, though it does take a little elbow grease. If you'd like to make your own and earn extra credit, here's a go-to recipe that I've used countless times.

Homemade Mayonnaise

Makes about ¾ cup

The key to fabulous homemade mayonnaise is a little bit of water and your willingness to whisk. To make sure I have the freshest oil, I buy a very small bottle of canola oil each time I make mayonnaise. I like to place a wet paper towel under my mixing bowl so it won't slip and slide around while I'm adding oil and whisking like crazy.

1 large egg, at room temperature
2 teaspoons freshly squeezed lemon juice
1 teaspoon water
1 teaspoon Dijon mustard
⅛ teaspoon salt
¾ cup very fresh canola oil

Separate the egg. Place the yolk in a medium mixing bowl. Reserve the white for another use.

Whisk the yolk, lemon juice, water, Dijon mustard, and salt until well combined and starting to have a few bubbles. Very slowly (several drops at a time) add oil in a very thin stream while whisking constantly. Continue until all of the oil is incorporated.

Store in the refrigerator up to 1 week.

Note: For a faster option, an immersion blender is a great choice for making mayonnaise. Use the tall cylindrical measuring cup that came with the blender. Place the first five ingredients in the cup, insert the immersion blender, then pour in all of the oil. Turn on the blender. Blend until all the ingredients are incorporated.

One Point from Perfect

Pimento cheese is a magical comfort food of the South. I grew up eating commodity-made, not very flavorful pimento cheese at my grandmother's house along with things like Southern Pear Salad, with canned pears, mayo, and shredded cheddar cheese, and Broccoli Cornbread made from Jiffy-brand cornbread mix. That pimento cheese wasn't my favorite, so I was pretty indifferent to pimento cheese in general.

When my husband, Jeremy, and I opened the Sweet Grass Dairy Cheese Shop in 2010, it was mostly a retail store with just a few tables in the back for anyone who wanted a cheese and charcuterie board and a great glass of wine or craft beer. Quickly we realized that many people in town wanted a place to go to get cheese and wine, and we steadily took out retail cases to replace them with more tables. When we wanted to expand the menu to include some snacks and sandwiches, we got so many requests for pimento cheese that finally I went to Jeremy to ask him if he could come up with a recipe. He grew up in Ohio and didn't have any history of eating pimento cheese at all.

Talking to local customers, Jeremy realized that many people feel very strongly about their family's pimento cheese recipe. Some people swear by using cheddar cheese as the base, whereas others really like to start with smoked gouda. One point of agreement in our area is that Duke's mayo is the best mayo option. Jeremy knew that if he was going to make a pimento cheese recipe, it needed to be the highest quality pimento cheese possible. He decided to use our

Thomasville Tomme as the base. This was the very first cheese that he learned how to make at Sweet Grass Dairy, and it has proved to be a great vehicle for our grass-based milk. He wanted to keep the shred larger so that people could actually taste the flavor of the cheese. As a curious cook and lover of Spanish flavor profiles, Jeremy chose to use Piquillo peppers instead of the traditional pimentos, as well as a little smoked Spanish paprika, or *pimentón*, for an enhanced smoky and fire-roasted flavor. Lastly, he decided to use Duke's mayo for extra creaminess and some Dijon mustard for a little kick on the finish.

We entered our Pimento Cheese into the American Cheese Society's annual competition in 2016. It was amazing to get such great feedback and a gold medal with a score of 99 out of 100! As of now, we are the only pimento cheese producers that are not only making a final pimento cheese product but also the base cheese used in the recipe. It has been a fun product to add to our handcrafted cheese portfolio, as it helps tell the story of our location in the Deep South. And lastly, we love making cheeses that create a flavorful and joyful experience, so our pimento cheese is a very fulfilling and rewarding product to produce.

Jessica Little

Co-owner, Sweet Grass Dairy
Thomasville, Georgia

Chapter 3
Pimento Cheese Recipes

Tom's Sunshine Pimento Cheese

Makes 1½ cups

My grandmother, Tom, didn't use a grater or fancy tools for her pimento cheese. I'm not sure if she grew up without a grater or if she simply didn't want to bother with washing another item in the kitchen. I remember her setting her much-loved glass mixing bowl with a block of cheese in a sunny spot on her porch before making her pimento cheese. This was how she softened the cheese before working it into small pieces. My screened porch is a perfect place for me to re-create her masterpiece.

1 (8-ounce) block sharp cheddar cheese
¼ cup mayonnaise
3 tablespoons diced pimentos, drained
Dash of freshly ground pepper

Place the cheddar in a medium mixing bowl and let it sit in a warm, sunny location outside for 20 to 25 minutes or until very soft. You should be able to press a finger into the cheese and make an indentation.

Break the cheese into small pieces, rubbing your thumb and fingertips together (like when you're pinching salt to throw into a recipe or when you're thinking about more money. Stir in the mayonnaise, pimentos, and pepper.

Store in the refrigerator in an airtight container for up to 1 week.

Buffalo Blue Pimento Cheese

Makes 2½ cups

I make a warm Buffalo chicken dip for tailgates and Christmas Eve. It's one of those dips that are hard to walk away from. It's loaded with Buffalo sauce, melty cheese, and green onions and is served in a cast-iron skillet. Achieving the same crave-worthy flavors with pimento cheese is a triumph! I serve the pimento cheese with scoop-friendly corn chips and celery, just like the warm dip. My favorite Buffalo sauce to use is Frank's RedHot Original.

1 (8-ounce) block Colby Jack cheese
4 ounces sharp white cheddar cheese
4 ounces cream cheese, softened
1 (4-ounce) jar diced pimentos, drained and patted dry
¼ cup mayonnaise
¼ cup Buffalo-style hot sauce, plus extra for garnish
2 ounces blue cheese, crumbled
2 green onions, thinly sliced
Corn chips, for serving
Celery sticks, for serving

Grate the Colby Jack and white cheddar using the large holes of a box grater. Place the Colby Jack, cheddar, cream cheese, pimentos, mayonnaise, hot sauce, and blue cheese in a medium mixing bowl. Stir to combine. At serving time, top with green onions, sprinkle with extra Buffalo sauce if desired, and serve with corn chips and/or celery sticks.

Store in the refrigerator in an airtight container for up to 3 days.

Bread-and-Butter Pimento Cheese

Makes 3½ cups

Thick slices of bread-and-butter pickles were always on platters at my grandmother Tom's house surrounded by deviled eggs and potato salad. The mustard seeds mingled with the sweetness of allspice so that my taste buds were confused between sweet and savory. Tom's pickles have always been comforting to me, and they make me think of her every time I enjoy them. Adding chopped pickles and a little of their brine to pimento cheese gives a wonderful sweet tang to the spread. I like to shop for pickles in the refrigerated case, since they are often crunchier.

2 (8-ounce) blocks extra-sharp white cheddar cheese
4 ounces cream cheese, softened
½ cup roasted red bell pepper, drained and diced
½ cup chopped bread-and-butter pickles
⅓ cup mayonnaise
¼ cup bread-and-butter pickle brine
¼ teaspoon cayenne pepper
⅛ teaspoon freshly ground black pepper
⅛ teaspoon salt

Grate the cheddar using the large holes of a box grater. Place the cheddar, cream cheese, roasted red bell pepper, pickles, mayonnaise, pickle brine, cayenne pepper, black pepper, and salt in a medium mixing bowl. Stir to combine.

Store in the refrigerator in an airtight container for up to 4 days.

Cheese Pimento

Makes 3 cups

It's often that pimento cheese comes up in conversation between Southerners. Ba Steedman, a friend filled with personality and liveliness, told me about the pimento cheese she grew up on. Her mom, Helen Bishop Kelley, always called it "cheese pimento." She made her pimento cheese by first grating the cheese with a Mouli rotary grater. I use a new version of the vintage kitchen tool, made by Zyliss. The texture of the cheese is almost like snow. The very fine cheese, yellow mustard, and lemon juice make this a standout for both flavor and texture.

1 (8-ounce) block extra-sharp cheddar cheese
½ cup diced pimentos, slightly drained
¼ cup mayonnaise
¾ teaspoon freshly squeezed lemon juice
½ teaspoon yellow mustard

Finely grate the cheddar in a crank-style cheese grater. Combine the cheddar, pimentos, mayonnaise, lemon juice, and yellow mustard in a medium mixing bowl. Stir until very creamy.

Store in the refrigerator in an airtight container for up to 1 week. Let come to room temperature before serving.

Buttery Tea Sandwich Pimento Cheese

Makes 1½ cups

Pimento cheese with butter was often chosen as a spread for tea sandwiches thanks to the incomparable creaminess. Because of the butter content, it spreads best at room temperature. Another decadent way to enjoy this rich and cheesy spread is as a finishing butter. I love it on grilled corn on the cob and on top of a thick grilled pork chop. If using as a butter, process the pimento cheese in the food processor until smooth. The mixture can be shaped into a log and chilled. Simply slice before using.

1 (8-ounce) block extra-sharp cheddar cheese
4 tablespoons unsalted butter, softened
2 tablespoons diced pimentos, drained
2 tablespoons mayonnaise
¼ teaspoon crushed red pepper
⅛ teaspoon salt
⅛ teaspoon garlic powder

Grate the cheddar using the small holes of a box grater. Place the cheddar, butter, pimentos, mayonnaise, crushed red pepper, salt, and garlic powder in a medium mixing bowl. Stir to combine.

Store in the refrigerator in an airtight container for up to 1 week.

Chipotle Pimento Cheese

Makes 1½ cups

Chipotle peppers, which are smoked jalapeños, come packed in adobo sauce in cans. Both the peppers and the sauce are incredible when added to pimento cheese recipes. It's not often that I can use an entire can of chipotles at one time, so I separate them on a parchment-lined sheet pan, freeze them, and seal them in a ziplock bag. Then I can always reach for one pepper to use in another recipe. Spread this hotter version on sturdy or hearty crackers and everyone will be asking for the recipe.

1 (8-ounce) block extra-sharp cheddar cheese
1 (2-ounce) jar diced pimentos, drained
⅓ cup mayonnaise
1 chipotle pepper packed in adobo sauce, diced
½ teaspoon adobo sauce
2 teaspoons finely chopped flat-leaf parsley
¼ teaspoon salt

Grate the cheddar using the large holes of a box grater. Place the cheddar, pimentos, mayonnaise, chipotle pepper, adobo sauce, parsley, and salt in a medium mixing bowl. Stir to combine.

Store in the refrigerator in an airtight container for up to 1 week.

Fried Dill Pickle Pimento Cheese

Makes 3 cups

It's easy. I adore fried pickles and I love pimento cheese. I set out to join the two together in hopes that I could create the ultimate spread. Corn chips are a perfect vessel for the nearly addictive cheesy recipe. Make sure to use dill pickle relish and not the more common sweet relish. The French-fried onions will be crunchier if you stir them in right before serving. Using just a tablespoon of ranch dressing mix will leave some in the envelope. I save the leftover mix in my spice cabinet for sprinkling on popcorn.

1 (8-ounce) block extra-sharp cheddar cheese
1 (8-ounce) package cream cheese, softened
1 (4-ounce) jar diced pimentos, drained
⅓ cup dill pickle relish, undrained
¼ cup mayonnaise
1 tablespoon ranch dressing mix
⅓ cup French-fried onions, plus more for garnish

Grate the cheddar using the large holes of a box grater. Place the cheddar, cream cheese, pimentos, pickle relish, mayonnaise, dressing mix, and fried onions in a medium mixing bowl. Stir to combine.

Store in the refrigerator in an airtight container for up to 4 days.

Fancy Pimento Cheese

Makes 4 cups

I've always thought that the more colorful pimento cheese is, the prettier it looks. This version is bursting with color, texture, and flavor. The two colors of bell peppers are important to the look. If you can only find green bell peppers, use bottled roasted peppers instead. There's one vegetable I never cook: green bell peppers.

1 red bell pepper
1 orange bell pepper
1 (8-ounce) block extra-sharp white cheddar
1 (8-ounce) block extra-sharp yellow cheddar
½ cup chopped pecans, toasted
4 green onions, thinly sliced
½ jalapeño, seeded and minced
3 tablespoons chopped flat-leaf parsley
⅓ cup mayonnaise
1 tablespoon dill pickle juice

Preheat the broiler.

Cut the bell peppers in half lengthwise; discard the seeds and membranes. Place the halves, skin side up, on a foil-lined sheet pan and flatten them with your hand. Broil for 8 minutes or until totally blackened. Wrap the bell peppers in foil and let stand for 10 minutes. Remove and discard the blackened skins. Chop the peppers.

Shred both cheddars on the large holes of a box grater. Place the cheddars, bell peppers, pecans, green onions, jalapeño, parsley, mayonnaise, and pickle juice in a large mixing bowl. Stir to combine.

Store in the refrigerator in an airtight container for up to 1 week.

Fine Parmesan and Pimentos

Makes 1¼ cups

The sharpness of aged Parmesan marries perfectly with the richness of olive oil and the zing of lemon. The cheese becomes almost as melt-in-your-mouth as a snowflake when grated with a Microplane zester. Best served at room temperature, this spread is especially good stuffed inside dates or on slices of fennel or hearty crackers. With no mayonnaise, it's less prone to spoilage and is thus a perfect choice for a picnic or tailgate.

7 ounces Parmigiano-Reggiano, plus extra for garnish
1 (4-ounce) jar diced pimentos, drained and patted dry
¼ cup extra virgin olive oil
2 tablespoons freshly squeezed lemon juice
2 tablespoons flat-leaf parsley, chopped
½ teaspoon crushed red pepper

Very finely grate the Parmigiano-Reggiano using a zester or the fine holes on a box grater. (I used a Microplane for testing.) The cheese should have the texture of freshly fallen snow.

Place the cheese, pimentos, olive oil, lemon juice, parsley, and crushed red pepper in a medium mixing bowl. Stir to combine. Allow to sit for 30 minutes before serving. Garnish with a fresh grating of Parmigiano-Reggiano if desired.

Store in the refrigerator in an airtight container for up to 1 week.

Gouda Prosciutto Pimento Cheese

Makes 4 cups

I haven't found anything that I don't like with prosciutto. I love the saltiness of it combined with gouda. Most prosciutto comes packaged with strips of paper separating the slices. It's a lot easier to chop once it's cold. Remove the paper strips, stack the slices and put them in the freezer for fifteen minutes before chopping. Gouda is most often made with cow's milk, but sometimes you'll see sheep's milk gouda at the cheese counter. I prefer cow's milk for this recipe.

4 ounces gouda cheese
4 ounces sharp white cheddar cheese
4 tablespoons diced pimentos, drained
⅓ cup mayonnaise
3 tablespoons finely chopped toasted pecans
½ teaspoon fresh oregano, chopped
3 ounces prosciutto, chopped

Grate the gouda and cheddar using the large holes of a box grater. Place the cheeses, pimentos, mayonnaise, pecans, oregano, and prosciutto in a medium mixing bowl. Stir to combine.

Store in the refrigerator in an airtight container for up to 4 days.

Hoop Pimento Cheese

Makes 2¼ cups

Hoop cheese (see text box on page 18) was some of the first cheese that Southerners used for pimento cheese. Until the 1950s, small-town stores made and sold their own hoop-shaped cheeses, but the short shelf life contributed to their disappearance. The hoop cheese mass-produced today is a bit of a cross between a mild cheddar and Monterey Jack. If you ever see small-batch hoop cheese available in a country store, buy it and give it a try.

I like to grate the onion on the same holes that I use for shredding the hoop cheese.

8 ounces hoop cheese
⅓ cup mayonnaise
1 (4-ounce) jar diced pimentos, drained
2 tablespoons grated Vidalia onion
¾ teaspoon white vinegar
¼ teaspoon salt
⅛ teaspoon freshly ground pepper

Remove the wax coating from hoop cheese. Grate the cheese using the large holes of a box grater. Place the hoop cheese, mayonnaise, pimentos, onion, vinegar, salt, and pepper in a medium mixing bowl. Stir to combine.

Store in the refrigerator in an airtight container for up to 1 week.

Jalapeño Popper Pimento Cheese

Makes 3½ cups

One of my favorite snacks to make at the beach is jalapeño poppers that I wrap in bacon and put on the grill. This recipe re-creates that same comforting spiciness in a pimento cheese. If you like even more spice, bump up the heat with different types of peppered cheese. In specialty markets, you can find habanero Jack and even Carolina Reaper cheddar. I know it's a lot of bacon, but please trust me.

This recipe is also just as good as a warm dip with tortilla or corn chips. Simply spread pimento cheese in a small ovenproof dish and bake at 350°F for about twenty minutes or until warmed through and very creamy.

- 2 (8-ounce) blocks pepper Jack cheese
- 4 ounces cream cheese, softened
- ½ cup sour cream
- 1 (4-ounce) jar diced pimentos, drained
- 2 tablespoons mayonnaise
- ⅛ teaspoon salt
- 8 ounces bacon, cooked and crumbled

Grate the pepper Jack using the large holes of a box grater. Combine the pepper Jack, cream cheese, sour cream, pimentos, mayonnaise, and salt in a medium mixing bowl. Stir in the bacon.

Store in the refrigerator in an airtight container for up to 4 days.

Layered Pimento Cheese

Serves 10 to 12

Channeling Spanish flavors and a much more polished look for pimento cheese, I used a loaf pan to shape this into a four-layer smoky spread. Use enough plastic wrap so there's plenty to fold back over to cover the top of the pan. Because it's easily contained in the pan, it's perfect to transport to parties and holidays for a festive spread. Just unmold it when you arrive and let it sit to soften.

1 (8-ounce) block sharp white cheddar cheese
1 (8-ounce) package cream cheese, softened
2 tablespoons chopped flat-leaf parsley
¼ teaspoon garlic powder
⅛ teaspoon dry mustard
1 (16-ounce) jar roasted red bell pepper strips, drained well
⅓ cup panko (Japanese-style breadcrumbs)
¾ teaspoon smoked paprika
¼ teaspoon cayenne pepper
¼ cup sliced almonds, toasted
Crackers, for serving

Cut the cheddar into ½-inch cubes. Transfer the cubes to a food processor. Pulse until very finely chopped. Add the cream cheese, parsley, garlic powder, and dry mustard. Process until combined. Remove the cheese mixture from the processor bowl and set it aside. Wash the bowl and blade well.

Combine the red bell pepper strips, panko, smoked paprika, and cayenne pepper in the cleaned food processor bowl. Pulse until finely chopped.

Line a loaf pan with plastic wrap. Spread half of the pepper mixture in the bottom of the pan. Spread half of the cheese mixture over the peppers, working carefully to avoid mixing the layers. Top with the remaining peppers and another layer of the cheese mixture. Cover and chill for 8 hours.

Turn the loaf pan upside down on a rectangular platter and peel the plastic wrap off the molded pimento cheese. The pepper layer will be on top. Sprinkle almonds over the top before serving. Allow to sit at room temperature for 15 minutes before serving. Serve as a spread with crackers.

Buttermilk Pimento Cheese

Makes 3 cups

Buttermilk in pimento cheese recipes can be found in older recipes and community cookbooks quite often. The tanginess is lovely with the cheese, and it adds a nice, slightly looser, texture.

I first tested this recipe before having friends over, and everyone literally raved. I had several people wanting a copy before I had even typed it up. It's that good. Make sure to look for whole buttermilk, and give it a good shake before using. It makes the pimento cheese much creamier than the reduced-fat versions.

- 2 (8-ounce) blocks extra-sharp cheddar cheese
- 1 cup roasted red bell peppers, drained
- 3 green onions, thinly sliced
- ⅓ cup whole buttermilk
- 2 tablespoons mayonnaise
- ⅛ teaspoon cayenne pepper
- ⅛ teaspoon freshly ground black pepper

Grate the cheddar using the large holes of a box grater. Slice the peppers into thin strips about 1 inch long. Place the cheddar, peppers, green onions, buttermilk, mayonnaise, cayenne pepper, and black pepper in a medium mixing bowl. Stir to combine.

Store in the refrigerator in an airtight container for up to 1 week.

Mimi's Pimento Cheese

Makes 3 cups

My mom was always my mom until I had babies. Then, as if overnight, she became "Mimi" for all of us, even my husband. If I slip and mention one of my parents as "Mom" or "Dad," my children look at me in total confusion as if I have no parents of my own. For Camden and Adair, the Dopsons only have a role as grandparents, and no other name exists anymore. I would have it no other way. Mimi and Papa are ready at any call for help, a ride to a friend's house, or even braiding a ponytail.

Mimi made pimento cheese for us all the time when we were growing up. It was basic, but really, really good. You'll hear women whisper about So-and-So's secret to pimento cheese, and a lot of times it's a mention of Worcestershire. Mimi's favorite use of her pimento cheese is to add it to her tomato sandwich.

2 (8-ounce) blocks sharp cheddar cheese
¾ cup mayonnaise
1 (4-ounce) jar diced pimento, drained
¼ teaspoon garlic powder
2 teaspoons Worcestershire sauce

Grate the cheddar using the large holes of a box grater. Place the cheddar, mayonnaise, pimento, garlic powder, and Worcestershire in a medium mixing bowl. Stir to combine.

Store in the refrigerator in an airtight container for up to 1 week.

Lindsey's Pimento-less Cheese

Makes 4½ cups

Lindsey Payne and I almost crossed paths while in culinary school at Johnson & Wales University. It wasn't long after we moved to Athens that she opened Lindsey's Culinary Market and pimento-less cheese became a staple for a lot of Athenians. Although pimentos are absent, I was excited to include her recipe in this collection. When I asked her for the story about where the pimentos went, she told me that when she was about eight years old, she and her mom, Jane, were making pimento cheese to give as Christmas gifts. The recipe was almost done when they realized they had forgotten the pimentos. Lindsey and her brother admitted to their dislike of pimentos, and the accidental omission became the new tradition.

Like many pimento cheese recipes, this one is passed down. Mrs. Payne got the recipe from her friend Mary Luper in Knoxville, Tennessee. She then made it her own version without pimentos.

2 (8-ounce) blocks sharp cheddar cheese
2 large whole kosher dill pickles
¾ cup mayonnaise
¼ cup diced red onion
¼ cup chopped pecans, toasted

Grate the cheddar using the large holes of a box grater. Finely chop the dill pickles. Combine the cheddar, pickles, mayonnaise, onion, and pecans in a medium mixing bowl. Fold to blend the ingredients, making sure to leave plenty of texture.

Store in the refrigerator in an airtight container for up to 1 week.

Miracle Whipped Pimento Cheese

Makes 1½ cups

The mayonnaise-versus-Miracle Whip debate has been going on as long as jar lids have been opened. Miracle Whip is not mayonnaise, but it's beloved for a reason. When Kraft first marketed Miracle Whip in the 1930s, it was touted as a cross of mayonnaise and salad dressing. During the Depression, Miracle Whip was advertised as a cheaper alternative to mayonnaise. It's actually lower in fat and calories than mayonnaise. I like that it adds flavor and richness at the same time. Thanks to being so spreadable and smooth, it makes lovely tea sandwiches. The white cheddar will turn a pretty color of light orange, thanks to the pimentos.

1 small garlic clove
1 (8-ounce) block sharp white cheddar cheese
1 (4-ounce) jar diced pimentos, drained
2 tablespoons mayonnaise
3 tablespoons Miracle Whip
¼ teaspoon salt
⅛ teaspoon freshly ground pepper

Process the garlic in a food processor fitted with the blade attachment until finely chopped.

Cut the cheddar into 1-inch cubes. Add the cheddar, pimento, mayonnaise, Miracle Whip, salt, and pepper to the food processor. Process until smooth, about 1 minute.

Store in the refrigerator in an airtight container for up to 1 week.

Mozzarella and Prosciutto Pimento Cheese

Makes 1¾ cups

I love this pimento cheese for its spreadability and for the saltiness from the prosciutto. Use a block of mozzarella from the cheese section, not fresh mozzarella. The food processor gives it a wonderfully smooth texture that's perfectly spreadable on a sandwich.

I almost always eat lunch alone, since everyone in my house is at school or at work. The day I tested this recipe, I made myself a grilled sandwich of pimento cheese on sourdough. It was raining outside, I warmed up some tomato soup to go with it, and it was an incredible meal. It was so good, I hated that I was the only one who got to enjoy it.

1 (8-ounce) block mozzarella cheese
2 ounces prosciutto, chopped
¼ cup mayonnaise
¼ cup roasted red bell peppers, drained and chopped
1½ teaspoons chopped fresh rosemary
⅛ teaspoon freshly ground black pepper

Cut the mozzarella into 1-inch cubes. Combine the mozzarella, prosciutto, mayonnaise, bell peppers, rosemary, and black pepper in the bowl of a food processor fitted with the blade. Pulse until the texture is spreadable.

Store in the refrigerator in an airtight container for up to 4 days.

Mrs. Hunnicutt's Pimento Cheese

Makes 3 cups

When you write a book about pimento cheese, you naturally hear who makes really good pimento cheese. It's a topic of conversation for me almost everywhere I go. I was volunteering in the kitchen at church when I heard about a neighbor who has a pimento cheese recipe that calls for using a mixer for five minutes to make the pimento cheese fluffy. (Pictured on page 4.) There was even discussion of whether this could actually be true. Well, it was. Theresa Hunnicutt lives up the river from us and learned to make pimento cheese from her mother, Virginia Burt, while growing up in Warm Springs, Georgia. After Mrs. Burt brought a batch to a neighborhood garden club meeting, her recipe gained a solid group of admirers. Mrs. Burt said the secret was the sugar. I think the five-minute marathon in the mixer is the real secret.

2 (8-ounce) blocks sharp cheddar cheese
1 (4-ounce) jar diced pimentos, drained
1 cup mayonnaise
1 teaspoon sugar
½ teaspoon salt

Grate the cheddar using the large holes of a box grater. Combine the cheddar, pimentos, mayonnaise, sugar, and salt in the bowl of a stand mixer fitted with the paddle attachment. Mix on low speed for 5 minutes.

Store in the refrigerator in an airtight container for up to 1 week.

Olive Pimento Cheese

Makes 4 cups

One of the first pimento cheese recipes I ever made on my own was loaded with pimento-stuffed green olives. I was in middle school and had been going through my mom's cookbooks looking for things to make. I remember cutting the olives in half and how pretty they were in the cheese. I was so proud of myself. To this day, I love pimento cheese with olives. It's a perfect combination.

1 (8-ounce) block extra-sharp cheddar cheese
1 (8-ounce) block sharp white cheddar cheese
1 cup pimento-stuffed green olives, chopped
¾ cup mayonnaise
2 green onions, thinly sliced
1 (4-ounce) jar diced pimentos, drained
⅛ teaspoon freshly ground pepper

Grate the cheddar cheeses using the large holes of a box grater. Place the cheeses, olives, mayonnaise, green onions, pimentos, and pepper in a medium mixing bowl. Stir to combine.

Store in the refrigerator in an airtight container for up to 1 week.

No-Mayo Pimento Cheese

Makes 2¼ cups

I like to use goat cheese for many things, so I tend to always have it on hand—so much so that I buy it at Costco to make sure I don't run out. It makes surprisingly creamy pimento cheese without the need for mayonnaise. It's a great "starter" version of pimento cheese for those who think they don't like mayonnaise (a condition that normally disappears with good Southern food). Make sure to avoid the flavored versions of goat cheese for this recipe.

1 (8-ounce) block extra-sharp cheddar cheese
4 ounces cream cheese, softened
4 ounces goat cheese, softened
3 tablespoons whole milk
1 (4-ounce) jar diced pimentos, well drained and patted dry
½ teaspoon salt
⅛ teaspoon freshly ground pepper

Grate the cheddar using the large holes of a box grater. Place the cheddar, cream cheese, goat cheese, and milk in the bowl of a stand mixer fitted with the paddle attachment. Mix until creamy and fully combined, about 30 seconds. Add the pimento, salt, and pepper. Mix for 30 seconds.

Store in the refrigerator in an airtight container for up to 1 week.

Pickled Jalapeño and Queso Fresco Pimento Cheese

Makes 2 cups

Spicy and salty have come together for a unique pimento cheese blend. Use your fingertips to break up the queso fresco into fine crumbles. This will ensure the dry Mexican cheese is evenly distributed throughout the spread. I love this version on hamburgers and hot dogs for a spicy kick. My parents (the lucky taste testers for all of my projects) took home this batch and raved about how good it was as a topping on their green salad.

1 (8-ounce) block extra-sharp cheddar cheese
4 ounces queso fresco, finely crumbled
1 (4-ounce) jar diced pimentos, drained
⅓ cup mayonnaise
¼ cup diced pickled jalapeños
¼ teaspoon ancho chili powder
¼ teaspoon salt

Grate the cheddar using the large holes of a box grater. Combine the cheddar, queso fresco, pimentos, mayonnaise, pickled jalapeños, chili powder, and salt in a medium mixing bowl. Stir well.

Store in the refrigerator in an airtight container for up to 1 week.

Pickled-Okra-Packed Pimento Cheese

Makes 2½ cups

I can't think of a thing I've made with pickled okra that didn't turn out wonderfully. And this is no exception. Even while I was testing pimento cheese recipes day in and day out, this is one of the recipes that I would keep coming back to just for snacking. Talk O'Texas is my favorite brand of pickled okra and is readily available in most grocery stores. The mild version is perfect.

Letting the pimento cheese chill before serving allows time for more pickle flavor to develop.

1 (8-ounce) block medium cheddar cheese
⅓ cup mayonnaise
¼ cup diced pimentos, drained
2 teaspoons Worcestershire sauce
1 small shallot, diced
¼ teaspoon cayenne pepper
¼ teaspoon salt
12 pods pickled okra, drained and thinly sliced (¾ cup)

Grate the cheddar using the large holes of a box grater. Place the cheddar, mayonnaise, pimentos, Worcestershire, shallot, cayenne pepper, and salt in a medium mixing bowl. Stir to combine. Fold in pickled okra until well distributed. Chill for 2 hours before serving.

Store in the refrigerator in an airtight container for up to 1 week.

"Plains Special" Cheese Ring

Makes 3 ½ cups cheese (serves 10)

First Lady Rosalynn Carter was known for her Southern hospitality in the Georgia governor's mansion, in the White House, and even at a cruising altitude of 30,000 feet. At her memorial service, her grandson Jason Carter told the story of a family trip that involved pimento cheese in the back of one of Delta's planes. Mrs. Carter brought a Tupperware of pimento cheese and a loaf of bread. She made each of the grandchildren a sandwich and then served others on the plane with what she had left. If that's not the epitome of a Southern woman, I don't know what is.

The National Archives published her famous cheese ring recipe. The sweet strawberry preserves and the bite from the grated onions are matched perfectly. Of all the times I have made her historic recipe, I have literally never had even a tablespoon left over. Mrs. Carter made her version in a ring mold, but I love the scalloped look that a brioche mold creates.

2 (8-ounce) blocks sharp cheddar cheese
1 small white onion
1 cup pecans, toasted and finely chopped
1 cup mayonnaise
¼ teaspoon freshly ground black pepper
⅛ teaspoon cayenne pepper
High-quality strawberry preserves
Crackers

Grate the cheddar using the large holes of a box grater. Grate the onion using the large holes of a box grater (you should have about ½ cup grated onion). Place the cheddar, onion, pecans, mayonnaise, black pepper, and cayenne pepper in a medium mixing bowl. Stir to combine.

Line a 5-cup brioche mold with plastic wrap. Wrap a small juice glass in plastic wrap. Lightly spray the inside of the mold and the outside of the glass with nonstick cooking spray. Place the glass upside down in the middle of the brioche mold to create a ring. Fill the mold with the cheese mixture. Cover and chill for 8 hours. May be stored in the refrigerator for up to 3 days.

When ready to serve, unmold onto a platter and gently remove the juice glass. Fill the center of the ring with strawberry preserves before serving. Serve with crackers.

Note: Don't worry if you don't own a brioche mold or ring mold for making a cheese ring. An easy substitution is a small, shallow mixing bowl with a small juice glass placed in the center.

Pickled Jalapeño Pimento Cheese

(Pictured on page 78)

Makes 4 cups

We are a family that tends to put pickled jalapeños on everything. I buy obnoxiously large jars at the grocery store so we'll never be faced with running out. I love them on cheeseburgers, chicken salad, hash browns, guacamole, pretty much everything. Make sure you pick up a jar of the spicy ones, not the sweet ones. The sweet-hot versions have their merits, but not here.

2 (8-ounce) blocks extra-sharp cheddar cheese
¾ cup roasted red peppers, finely chopped
½ cup mayonnaise
¼ cup chopped pickled jalapeños, plus extra slices for garnish
2 tablespoons finely chopped Vidalia onion

Grate the cheddar cheese using the large holes of a box grater. Place the cheddar, red peppers, mayonnaise, jalapeños, and onion in a medium mixing bowl. Stir to combine.

Store in the refrigerator in an airtight container for up to 1 week.

Pimento Cheese with Pepper Jelly and Bacon

Makes 3½ cups

I have a friend in Athens, Crystal Leach, who makes the world's best pepper jelly. I've unsuccessfully tried many times to make jelly that can hold a candle to hers. It doesn't look difficult, but only the most talented canners can convince all of the pepper pieces to float evenly throughout the jar, as if suspended by magic. I often will add her pepper jelly to pimento cheese and bacon sandwiches. Combining the three Southern favorites into one pimento cheese is nothing short of dreamy. Look for pepper jelly locally, but if you buy your pepper jelly from the grocery store, avoid the green-colored versions.

1 (8-ounce) block extra-sharp cheddar cheese
1 (8-ounce) block white cheddar cheese
2 slices thick-cut bacon, cooked and crumbled
1 (4-ounce) jar diced pimentos, drained
⅓ cup mayonnaise
⅓ cup pepper jelly

Grate the cheddar cheeses using the large holes of a box grater. Place the cheeses, bacon, pimentos, mayonnaise, and pepper jelly in a medium mixing bowl. Stir to combine.

Store in the refrigerator in an airtight container for up to 4 days.

Pimento Cheese, Augusta National Style

Makes 3¼ cups

I'm married to an avid golfer. But when the opportunity arises to attend the world's most famous golf tournament, I mainly tag along for the pimento cheese sandwiches. The crazy-low price, the soft white bread, the legendary spread, the crinkly green sandwich wrappers all make for the most famous sandwich that exists. Thousands of cooks, maybe more, have tried to re-create the recipe. (See the last section of chapter 1 for the sordid history.) As a woman who has saved wrappers and pinned them in her office for more than fifteen years, I can say that almost every recipe I've seen for the spread was written by someone who has overthought the ingredients.

2 (8-ounce) blocks sharp cheddar cheese
¾ cup mayonnaise
6 tablespoons undrained diced pimentos
2 ounces cream cheese, softened
¼ teaspoon salt

Grate the cheddar using the large holes of a box grater. Combine the cheddar, mayonnaise, pimentos, cream cheese, and salt in the bowl of a stand mixer fitted with the paddle attachment. Mix on low speed for 1 minute.

Store in the refrigerator in an airtight container for up to 1 week.

Pimento Cheese with Chili Crunch

Makes 3¼ cups

Chili crunch makes almost everything better, including pimento cheese. Think of a crunchy mixture of pepper flakes, seeds, and crispy bits of goodness combined with oil. It's now widely available in grocery stores, and it's fun to find a brand and the level of heat you like. Chili crunch has a little more texture than chili crisp, but either will work great for this recipe. I've never met one I didn't like.

2 (8-ounce) blocks extra-sharp cheddar cheese
4 ounces cream cheese, softened
⅓ cup mayonnaise
1 (4-ounce) jar diced pimentos, undrained
¼ cup chili crunch, well stirred

Grate the cheddar using the large holes of a box grater. Combine the cheddar, cream cheese, mayonnaise, and pimentos in a medium mixing bowl.

Spread into a shallow serving bowl, but leave some texture so the pimento cheese isn't smooth on top. At serving time drizzle with about 1 tablespoon of chili crunch.

Store in the refrigerator, covered with plastic wrap, for 2 days. Let sit at room temperature for 25 minutes before serving.

Pimentos and Fontina Cheese

Makes 2 cups

This is one of the prettiest pimento cheeses and has a milder flavor than versions made with the classic cheddar. Fontina is slightly creamy, made with cow's milk, and has tiny holes called eyes. Look for it in the deli section of your grocery story. It melts really well, so grab some extra for a cheeseburger or your next casserole topping. If it's too soft for grating, place the cheese in the freezer for 10 minutes.

8 ounces fontina cheese
¼ cup mayonnaise
1 (4-ounce) jar diced pimentos, drained
2 tablespoons finely diced red onion
1 tablespoon chopped fresh parsley
¼ teaspoon sweet paprika
⅛ teaspoon smoked paprika
⅛ teaspoon salt
Dash of hot sauce

Grate the fontina using the large holes of a box grater. Place the fontina, mayonnaise, pimentos, onion, parsley, sweet paprika, smoked paprika, salt, and hot sauce in a medium mixing bowl. Stir to combine.

Store in the refrigerator in an airtight container for up to 1 week.

Secret Sauce Pimento Cheese

Makes 2 ½ cups

I'd never thought much about Durkee Famous Sauce until Covid crashed the world. During that time it was usual for me to receive calls and emails asking how to find an ingredient that was in short supply. I had no answer to where to find the sauce everyone was craving. It seemed that for fans of the sauce, it was just as hot a 2020 commodity as paper towels and toilet paper.

Southern women have been slipping their secret sauce into egg salads, pimento cheese, deviled eggs, and chicken salads for generations. If you're lucky, a loose-lipped grandmother will share with you that Durkee Famous Sauce is indeed the key to that recipe that everyone loves. The tangy sauce has been cherished by home cooks since it appeared at the Chicago World's Fair in 1933. It's the best blend of mustard and mayonnaise and vinegar. Look for it online if you can't find it in your local grocery store.

1 (8-ounce) block medium cheddar cheese
1 (4-ounce) jar diced pimentos, drained
2 tablespoons mayonnaise
2 tablespoons Durkee Famous Sauce
1 tablespoon diced shallot
2 tablespoons chopped flat-leaf parsley

Grate the cheddar using the large holes of a box grater. Place the cheddar, pimentos, mayonnaise, Durkee Famous Sauce, shallot, and parsley in a medium mixing bowl. Stir to combine.

Store in the refrigerator in an airtight container for up to 4 days.

Pineapple Pimento Cheese

Makes 2½ cups

Sherry Sheppard, a middle school teacher friend, first introduced me to the idea of pineapple in pimento cheese. I had never heard of it or, frankly, thought of it at all. Sherry's pimento cheese is one of her best recipes, and when she let me in on her secret ingredient, I was shocked to learn it was canned pineapple. When I mentioned this unexpected ingredient to a dear friend from St. Simons Island, Shelley Renner, she told me how her mother would add pineapple to pimento cheese to fancy it up for special occasions, calling it Easter Pimento Cheese.

I was amazed how beautifully the flavors work together in the extra creamy version. This is now one of my favorite ways to eat pimento cheese. The pineapple flavor is sweeter on the second day.

1 (8-ounce) block extra-sharp cheddar cheese
1 (8-ounce) can crushed pineapple in pineapple juice, undrained
⅓ cup roasted red bell pepper strips, drained and roughly chopped
4 ounces cream cheese, softened
2 tablespoons mayonnaise
¼ teaspoon salt
¼ teaspoon crushed red pepper, plus extra for garnish
Dash of cayenne pepper

Grate the cheddar using the large holes of a box grater. Place the cheddar, pineapple, bell pepper, cream cheese, mayonnaise, salt, crushed red pepper, and cayenne pepper in a medium mixing bowl. Stir to combine. Garnish with crushed red pepper.

Store in the refrigerator in an airtight container for up to 1 week.

Simple Pimento Cheese

Makes 3 cups

The most beloved pimento cheeses are often the simplest. That's one of the beauties of the South's most favorite spread. No fancy ingredients are needed. This is the version I make often when I'm in a hurry or am hit with a craving.

2 (8-ounce) blocks extra-sharp cheddar cheese
¾ cup mayonnaise
1 (4-ounce) jar diced pimentos, drained
2 tablespoons grated Vidalia onion

Grate the cheddar using the large holes of a box grater. Place the cheddar, mayonnaise, pimentos, and onion in a medium mixing bowl. Stir to combine.

Store in the refrigerator in an airtight container for up to 5 days.

Sriracha Pimento Cheese

(Pictured on page 78)

Makes 3¼ cups

If you love sriracha, you'll love this recipe. This favorite chili sauce originated in Thailand and is now on shelves at nearly every grocery store in America. It's not as hot as Tabasco and is tangy and just a little sweet. I like to finely shred the cheese for this recipe, since it helps the hot sauce to work into each and every shred of cheese. A food processor makes that task the easiest.

2 (8-ounce) blocks Colby Jack cheese
⅔ cup roasted red peppers, drained and chopped
½ cup chopped Vidalia onion
½ cup mayonnaise
3 tablespoons sriracha, plus extra for garnish

Grate the Colby Jack cheese using the fine holes of a box grater or the fine holes of a food processor blade. Place the cheese, peppers, onion, mayonnaise, and sriracha in a medium mixing bowl. Stir to combine. Sprinkle with more sriracha, if desired.

Store in the refrigerator in an airtight container for up to 4 days.

Inox France

Social Circle Pimento Cheese

(Pictured on page 78)

Makes 5 cups

This pimento cheese materialized as a result of using what needed to be used in Nathalie Dupree's kitchen (which doubled as her television studio) in Social Circle, Georgia. I spent a year becoming a "chicken" of Nathalie's, and she set me on the professional path that I still follow today. I can't imagine what my life would have been without her. I remember there was a new food processor (she always had the coolest new kitchen tools) and some cheddar that was just about to be out of date. She was always kind to let us experiment in the kitchen, as long as we were learning something valuable.

2 (8-ounce) blocks sharp cheddar cheese
1 (8-ounce) package cream cheese, softened
2 (4-ounce) jars diced pimento, drained
1 cup mayonnaise
½ red bell pepper, finely chopped
10 green olives, diced
2 tablespoons Worcestershire sauce
1 tablespoon finely chopped white onion
Freshly ground black pepper, to taste

Cut the cheddar into 1-inch cubes. Combine the cheddar, cream cheese, pimentos, mayonnaise, bell pepper, olives, Worcestershire, onion, and black pepper in the bowl of a food processor fitted with the metal blade. Process until creamy.

Store in the refrigerator in an airtight container for up to 1 week.

Tex-Mex Pimento Cheese

Makes 2¼ cups

I had some locally made pork rinds in the kitchen while I was testing this recipe. I fell head over heels in love with the spicy spread on top of the airy and crispy rinds. Ancho chili powder can be hard to find, so if you run across it in a grocery store, stock up. The fresh peppers, when diced, can release a little water. If needed, just dab the liquid with a paper towel.

1 (8-ounce) block extra-sharp cheddar cheese
1 jalapeño pepper, seeded and diced
1 Anaheim pepper, seeded and diced
1 (4-ounce) jar diced pimentos, drained
2 green onions, thinly sliced
½ cup mayonnaise
½ teaspoon ancho chili powder
¼ teaspoon salt
⅛ teaspoon cayenne pepper
Chopped fresh cilantro, for garnish

Grate the cheddar using the large holes of a box grater. Place the cheddar, diced jalapeño and Anaheim peppers, pimentos, green onions, mayonnaise, chili powder, salt, and cayenne pepper in a medium mixing bowl. Stir to combine. Garnish with fresh cilantro, if desired.

Store in the refrigerator in an airtight container for up to 3 days.

White Pimento Cheese

Makes 4 cups

Three cheeses give a depth of flavor to this pimento cheese and its pale color. This version is insanely good as a dip for veggies. Use a block of mozzarella from the cheese section, not fresh mozzarella. I like to serve this pimento cheese with a couple of other flavors as a tasting-type appetizer.

1 (8-ounce) block sharp white cheddar cheese
4 ounces extra-sharp cheddar cheese
4 ounces mozzarella cheese
1 (4-ounce) jar diced pimentos, drained
1 cup mayonnaise
½ cup finely chopped toasted pecans

Grate the cheddar cheeses and mozzarella using the large holes of a box grater. Place the cheeses, pimentos, mayonnaise, and pecans in a large mixing bowl. Stir to combine.

Store in the refrigerator in an airtight container for up to 1 week.

Lemony Goat Pimento Cheese

Makes 1 cup

With the lighter and tangier addition of Greek yogurt, this high cotton version of a classic is a pleasant surprise. It's wonderful spread on slices of raw vegetables, especially cucumber. When shopping for plain Greek yogurt, read carefully to avoid accidentally coming home from the grocery story with vanilla flavored.

2 ounces sharp white cheddar cheese
4 ounces goat cheese, softened
2 tablespoons plain Greek yogurt
2 tablespoons diced pimento, drained and patted dry
½ teaspoon lemon zest
½ teaspoon honey
½ teaspoon chopped fresh thyme, plus more for garnish
Freshly ground pepper, for garnish

Grate the cheddar using the large holes of a box grater. Place the cheddar, goat cheese, yogurt, pimento, lemon zest, honey, and thyme in a medium mixing bowl. Stir to combine. Garnish with a sprig of thyme and pepper, if desired.

Store in an airtight container in the refrigerator for up to 4 days.

Smoky Pimento Cheese

Makes 3 cups

I started to love smoked gouda thanks to a potato gratin I make for Christmas with the rich and creamy smoked cheese. Using high-quality smoked cheeses makes all the difference. Look for them in the deli section of your grocery store. The edges of smoked gouda are a darker brown than the center of the cheese. Just grate everything, edges and all.

8 ounces smoked gouda
8 ounces smoked cheddar cheese
4 ounces cream cheese, softened
1 (4-ounce) jar diced pimentos, drained
⅓ cup mayonnaise
½ tablespoon Worcestershire sauce
¼ teaspoon sweet paprika
⅛ teaspoon salt
Pinch of cayenne pepper

Grate the gouda and cheddar using the large holes of a box grater. Place the gouda, cheddar, cream cheese, pimentos, mayonnaise, Worcestershire, paprika, salt, and cayenne pepper in a medium mixing bowl. Stir to combine.

Store in the refrigerator in an airtight container for up to 1 week.

Soul Nourishment

Homemade pimento cheese spread on a saltine cracker is close to my heart. When my father was ill in 1994, our family friend Margaret Milam arrived at our Nashville house with a tub of pimento cheese and a warm loaf of date nut bread. During happier times, when my older daughter graduated from college, her boyfriend's mother packed quart jars full of homemade pimento cheese into a cooler and drove them across four state lines to sustain us all graduation week. Good homemade pimento cheese isn't hard to make. And as a Depression food, its ingredients are humble. But we can embellish it and make it our own and let it nourish our souls and give us strength to carry on in those good times and bad.

Anne Byrn

Author of *Baking in the American South*
Nashville, Tennessee

Chapter 4
Stirring It In

Absolute, Incredible, Over-the-Top BLT Sandwiches

Makes 4 sandwiches

A good BLT is one of the highlights of summer. I don't remember ever turning one down. Making one with fried green tomatoes and adding pimento cheese takes it to a whole new level. Any pimento cheese will work in these sandwiches. I also like to add pepper jelly to this crazy-good sandwich.

FOR THE FRIED GREEN TOMATOES:

Canola oil, for frying
1 cup plain yellow cornmeal
1 cup all-purpose flour
1 teaspoon salt
½ teaspoon freshly ground pepper
2 large eggs, beaten
¼ cup whole buttermilk
2 large green tomatoes

Pour oil to a depth of ¼ inch in a large skillet; heat to 350°F over medium-high heat. Meanwhile, combine the cornmeal, flour, salt, and pepper in a large bowl. Combine the eggs and buttermilk in a small bowl.

Peel the tomatoes with a vegetable peeler and cut them into ½-inch-thick slices. Dredge the tomato slices in the cornmeal mixture, pressing to adhere. Dip the slices in the egg mixture, then repeat the dredging in the cornmeal mixture. Fry the tomatoes, in two batches, in the hot oil for 3 minutes on each side or until golden brown. Drain on a wire rack placed over a sheet pan.

FOR THE SANDWICHES:

⅔ cup pimento cheese
8 slices sourdough bread, toasted
4 lettuce leaves
8 slices Fried Green Tomatoes
8 slices bacon, cooked crisp

Spread pimento cheese over one side of each bread slice. On four of the bread slices, layer a lettuce leaf, 2 Fried Green Tomato slices, and 2 bacon slices. Cover with the remaining slices of bread, cheese side down.

Adair's Tomato and Pimento Cheese Pie

Serves 8

My daughter, Adair, and I always make tomato pies during the summer at the beach. It's easily her favorite food of the season. It's not a quick process, but it's worth every minute. Don't skip the step of letting the tomatoes sit on the paper towels to dry. Otherwise the pie can be too watery and not slice cleanly when coming out of the pie plate. I like to use the store-brand refrigerated piecrusts from Publix. They taste the closest to homemade that I've found.

½ (15-ounce) package refrigerated piecrusts
2¼ pounds heirloom tomatoes
½ teaspoon salt
8 ounces bacon
1 white onion, cut into thin strips
1 (8-ounce) block extra-sharp cheddar cheese
1 (4-ounce) jar diced pimentos, drained and patted dry
⅔ cup chopped fresh basil
½ cup mayonnaise
1 teaspoon Dijon mustard
½ teaspoon freshly ground pepper, divided
1 large egg, beaten

Preheat the oven to 400°F.

Roll a piecrust on a lightly floured surface to a 14-inch circle. Line a 9-inch deep dish pie plate with the crust. Fold the edges under and use two fingers to crimp. Use the tines of a fork to lightly pierce the crust. Line the piecrust with parchment paper and fill with dried beans or pie weights. Bake at 400°F for 15 minutes. Remove the parchment paper and weights; let the crust cool.

Slice the tomatoes into ⅓-inch-thick slices. Place them in a single layer on a sheet pan lined with several paper towels. Sprinkle the slices with the salt. Cover and lightly press with more paper towels to help absorb any extra liquid. Let sit.

Chop the bacon. Cook in a medium skillet over medium-low heat until crisp. Remove the bacon and drain on paper towels. Pour off all but one tablespoon of the drippings in the skillet. Reserve for another use. Cook the onion in the drippings over medium-low heat until the onion is very browned, about 10 minutes. Drain on paper towels.

Grate the cheddar using the large holes of a box grater. Combine the cheddar, pimentos, basil, mayonnaise, Dijon mustard, ¼ teaspoon of the pepper, and the egg in a medium mixing bowl. Stir until well blended. Fold in the reserved bacon and onion.

Remove the paper towels from the top of the sliced tomatoes and replace with new paper towels. Press slightly to absorb any extra moisture.

Spread one-third of the pimento cheese mixture in the bottom of the cooled piecrust. Layer with one-third of the sliced tomatoes. Repeat these layers twice, ending with tomato slices as the top layer of the pie. Sprinkle with the remaining ¼ teaspoon pepper.

Bake at 400°F for 40 minutes or until the filling is set. Let sit 1 hour before serving.

Buttermilk Hush Puppies Stuffed with Pimento Cheese

Makes 22

Growing up, we never had a fish fry without hush puppies and grits. It's possible that I love the crispy, browned round treats more than I care for even the best fresh fish. It's tempting to overfill pimento cheese on each scoop of dough, but keeping it small prevents it from escaping as it cooks.

4 ounces sharp cheddar cheese
1 tablespoon mayonnaise
1 (2-ounce) jar diced pimento, drained
Vegetable oil, for frying
2 ½ cups self-rising white cornmeal mix (I use White Lily's Buttermilk mix)
1 cup finely chopped onion
1 teaspoon sugar
1 ¼ cups whole buttermilk
1 large egg, beaten

Grate the cheddar on the large holes of a box grater. Place the cheddar, mayonnaise, and pimento in a small bowl. Stir to combine.

Pour oil to a depth of 2 inches in a Dutch oven; heat to 375°F. Combine the cornmeal mix, onion, and sugar in a large bowl. Whisk the buttermilk and egg in a small bowl and add to the cornmeal mixture, stirring just until the dry ingredients are moistened.

Scoop out a scant tablespoonful of dough in a measuring spoon. Top with a teaspoonful of pimento cheese. Cover with another scant tablespoonful of dough, and use your fingers to mold it around the cheese on all sides. Repeat procedure with remaining dough and pimento cheese.

Frying in batches, carefully drop stuffed hush puppies into hot oil, and fry about 1½ minutes on each side or until lightly browned. Drain on a wire rack placed over a sheet pan. Serve immediately.

Charleston Pimento Cheese Dip

Serves 6

It's rare to find a Southern cook who hasn't served Charleston Cheese at a party. It's an heirloom recipe that's been around for nearly as long as cheese has been paired with crackers. Although you need only a few round buttery crackers for the topping, you'll want the rest of the box for enjoying my version of this classic.

1 (8-ounce) block extra-sharp cheddar cheese
1 (8-ounce) package cream cheese, softened
1 (4-ounce) jar diced pimentos, drained and patted dry
⅓ cup mayonnaise
3 green onions, thinly sliced
1 jalapeño, seeded and diced
¼ teaspoon hot sauce
8 round buttery crackers, plus more for serving
4 thick-cut bacon slices, cooked and crumbled

Preheat the oven to 350°F.

Grate the cheddar using the large holes of a box grater. Place the cheddar, cream cheese, pimentos, mayonnaise, green onions, jalapeño, and hot sauce in a medium mixing bowl. Stir to combine.

Spread the mixture into a 9-inch pie plate. Crumble the crackers over the cheese mixture.

Bake uncovered at 350°F for 15 minutes. Top with bacon before serving. Serve warm with buttery round crackers.

Cornbread Omelets with Pimento Cheese and Bacon

Makes 4 omelets

For those of us who cook for a living, adventures with friends often revolve around food. My good friend Mary Moore and I took a road trip to Tennessee to be judges at Lodge's National Cornbread Festival (and to hang with Mark Kelly of Lodge Cast Iron). It's very fair to say we consumed more than our share of cornbread and festive libations. Luckily there was a nearly magical cure offered on the breakfast menu. I'd never heard of cornbread omelets until then, but have thought about them a thousand times since being in cornbread heaven on the banks of the Tennessee River. Add whatever filling you like. The pimento cheese and bacon can be just the start. I especially like Pickled Jalapeño Pimento Cheese (page 66) for this recipe.

8 slices bacon
1 cup whole milk
1 large egg
1 cup self-rising white cornmeal mix (I use White Lily's Buttermilk mix)
1 ⅓ cups pimento cheese

Cut the bacon slices in half lengthwise. Cook until crisp, in batches, in an 8-inch nonstick skillet. Drain on paper towels. Pour off most of the drippings, leaving about 1 tablespoon in the skillet. Set the remaining drippings aside.

Whisk the milk, egg, cornmeal mix, and 2 tablespoons of the reserved bacon drippings in a medium mixing bowl.

Heat the skillet with bacon drippings over medium-low heat. For each omelet, pour about ½ cup cornmeal batter into the skillet. Cook for 90 seconds. Carefully flip the omelet. Spread ⅓ cup pimento cheese on half of the omelet circle in the skillet. Top with 2 strips of bacon. Turn the omelet out onto a plate, folding over in the process so the cornbread forms a traditional half circle.

Repeat for remaining omelets.

Country Ham Jam with Pimento Cheese and Crackers

Makes 2 cups

If pimento cheese was looking for a lifelong meaty bedfellow, this would be it. Choose any pimento cheese you like and your favorite crackers for a pairing that everyone will be raving about. I often take this to parties as a starter with cocktails, and I always come home with empty platters.

1 pound country ham, finely chopped (about 3 cups)
2 cups chopped Vidalia onion
5 garlic cloves, minced
½ cup firmly packed light brown sugar
1 cup Coca-Cola, divided
1 tablespoon plus 2 teaspoons cider vinegar
1 teaspoon dried thyme
2 tablespoons unsalted butter
1 tablespoon bourbon
½ teaspoon freshly ground pepper
Pimento cheese
Sturdy crackers or crostini

Cook the ham in a large skillet over medium heat for 3 minutes, stirring occasionally. Add the onion and garlic and sauté for 5 minutes or until the onions are tender. Add the brown sugar and stir to coat the ham. Add ½ cup of the Coca-Cola and the cider vinegar and thyme. Bring to a boil, reduce the heat to low, and simmer, stirring occasionally, for 30 minutes. (If the mixture gets too dry, add a tablespoon of water.)

Add the remaining ½ cup Coca-Cola and simmer for 30 minutes, stirring occasionally. Remove from the heat. Stir in the butter, bourbon, and pepper. Allow to cool for 30 minutes.

Pulse in a food processor until the ham is finely chopped and the mixture is spreadable. Serve immediately, or store in the refrigerator in an airtight container for up to 1 week. Allow to sit at room temperature for 20 minutes before serving.

Serve with pimento cheese and crackers.

Dates Stuffed with Pimento Cheese

Makes about 22 dates

I learned how dreamy a date stuffed with cheese can be from Athens chef Peter Dale, who made dates stuffed with Manchego, one of my hometown's favorite appetizers. The only problem is that it's nearly impossible to eat just one. You can use just about any pimento cheese for this recipe. I tested with Buttermilk Pimento Cheese (page 50).

12 ounces pitted Medjool dates (about 22 dates)
5 celery ribs
½ cup pimento cheese
Smoked paprika, for garnish

Pitted dates should be sliced on one side lengthwise, so you can open them up like a book.

Cut each celery rib into 3 strips lengthwise. Then cut each strip into 2½-inch pieces.

In each opened date, stuff 2 strips of celery and then top with about 1 teaspoon of pimento cheese. Arrange on a platter and sprinkle with paprika.

Grilled Pimento Cheese and Ham Sandwiches

Makes 4 sandwiches

I've never met a person who didn't love a grilled cheese sandwich. And if I do, it's likely we won't be friends. I also associate grilled cheese with rainy days, and it's one reason I cherish cold, damp days at home in the winter. Use any pimento cheese here. One of my favorites is Bread-and-Butter Pimento Cheese (page 36).

3 tablespoons unsalted butter, softened
8 slices multigrain bread
2 cups pimento cheese
⅓ pound deli ham, thinly sliced

Spread butter on one side of each bread slice. Place the bread slices, buttered side down, on waxed paper. Spread ¼ cup of the pimento cheese on each slice of bread. Arrange ham slices evenly on four slices of bread. Top with the remaining bread slices, buttered side up.

Cook the sandwiches in a large skillet or griddle over medium heat, 2 to 3 minutes on each side, or until the sandwiches are golden brown and the pimento cheese is melty.

Herbed Pimento Cheese Frittata

Serves 6

Frittatas are just as good for supper as they are for breakfast. Either time of day, this one is quick and very beautiful right out of the oven. Add a salad and a meal is made. Make sure your skillet is ovenproof before putting it under the broiler.

10 large eggs
½ cup whole milk
½ teaspoon salt
¼ teaspoon freshly ground black pepper
1 cup shredded extra-sharp cheddar cheese
2 tablespoons chopped fresh herbs (I use rosemary, basil, thyme, and sage)
1½ tablespoons olive oil
⅔ cup roasted red bell peppers, drained and chopped

Preheat the broiler.

Whisk the eggs, milk, salt, and black pepper in a medium mixing bowl until well combined. Stir in the cheddar and herbs.

Heat the olive oil in a 10-inch ovenproof nonstick skillet over medium heat. Add the roasted red bell peppers. Sauté for about 2 minutes. Stir the egg mixture to make sure the cheese is well incorporated and gently pour it over the peppers in the skillet. As it starts to cook, gently push a nonmetallic spatula along the bottom of the skillet to help the egg mixture cook all the way through. After about 2 minutes, cover and cook over low heat for 10 to 12 minutes to allow the top to set.

Broil 5 inches from the heat for 2 minutes or until golden. Cut into wedges. Serve immediately.

Macaroni and Pimento Cheese

Serves 8

I eat macaroni and cheese any chance I get. I never grew out of the obsession that most children have with the gooey, cheesy comfort food. Making it with extra-sharp cheddar, cream cheese, and pimentos combines two of my favorites in one of the richest casseroles ever.

1 (16-ounce) package elbow macaroni
10 ounces extra-sharp cheddar cheese
½ cup unsalted butter
½ cup all-purpose flour
4 cups whole milk
2 ounces cream cheese
2 teaspoons salt
½ teaspoon freshly ground pepper
1 (4-ounce) jar diced pimentos, drained

Preheat the oven to 350°F.

Prepare the macaroni according to package directions. Grate the cheddar using the large holes of a box grater and set aside.

Melt the butter in a large, heavy saucepan over low heat and whisk in the flour until smooth. Cook for 1 minute, whisking constantly. Gradually whisk in the milk and cook over medium heat, whisking constantly, for 5 minutes or until the mixture is thickened and bubbly.

Add the cheddar cheese, cream cheese, salt, and pepper, and stir until the cheeses melt. Stir in the pimentos and cooked macaroni.

Spoon the mixture into a lightly greased 13-by-9-inch baking dish. The baking dish will be very full. Place the baking dish on a sheet pan and bake at 350°F for 20 minutes or until thoroughly heated.

Pecan Pimento Cheese Ball

serves 8 to 10

If you grew up in the South, you likely grew up with cheese balls at family gatherings and holidays. When they started appearing on menus again a few years ago, I was thrilled! I like to divide to make two small versions so it's easy to replenish for guests. A mostly eaten cheese ball isn't pretty.

1 (8-ounce) package cream cheese, softened
6 ounces sharp cheddar cheese, shredded
3 tablespoons drained pimentos, patted dry
2 teaspoons finely chopped flat-leaf parsley
1 tablespoon minced shallot
1 teaspoon Worcestershire sauce
Dash of hot sauce
⅛ teaspoon salt
¾ cup finely chopped toasted pecans
Assorted crackers, for serving

Beat the cream cheese, cheddar, pimentos, parsley, shallot, Worcestershire, hot sauce, and salt with an electric mixer at medium speed until combined and creamy. Divide the cheese mixture in half. Shape each half into a ball.

Coat each ball with the pecans. Wrap loosely in waxed paper, seal in a plastic bag, and refrigerate for 2 hours (or up to 3 days) before serving. Serve with the crackers.

Pimento Cheese Buttermilk Biscuits

Makes 16 biscuits

My two grandmothers were from different areas of Georgia (north and south) and made totally different biscuits. One was cut from patted-out dough with a tomato paste can and was flaky; the other was a drop biscuit made to be slathered with butter. I now have a counter in my kitchen just for making biscuits. These are made even richer with cheese and pimentos in each bite. Try stuffing these biscuits with ham and softened butter for the ultimate brunch biscuit. Or just butter and pepper jelly for a treat.

2 cups self-rising soft-wheat flour (such as White Lily), plus extra for dusting the countertop
1 cup finely grated sharp cheddar cheese
1 teaspoon baking powder
¼ teaspoon salt
⅛ teaspoon freshly ground pepper
1 (4-ounce) jar diced pimentos, drained and patted very dry
¾ cup whole buttermilk

Preheat the oven to 425°F. Line a sheet pan with parchment paper.

Combine the flour, cheddar, baking powder, salt, and pepper in the bowl of a food processor fitted with the metal blade. Pulse until the cheese is very finely chopped. Add the pimentos and pulse four times. Add the buttermilk and pulse until the dough comes together and looks like a ball going around and around in the bowl.

Turn the dough out onto a well-floured surface. Using floured hands, knead the dough twice by folding it over and pressing down with the heels of your hands. If needed, sprinkle with a little flour to make a smooth dough. The dough should not be sticky.

Pat the dough to a ¾-inch thickness. Cut with a 2-inch round cutter. (Be very careful not to twist the cutter, to prevent lopsided biscuits.) Combine any dough scraps, again pat to a ¾-inch thickness, and cut into rounds. (Discard any remaining scraps.) Place the biscuits, with sides touching, on a parchment-lined sheet pan.

Bake at 425°F for 17 to 18 minutes or until lightly browned.

Pimento Cheese and Fried Oyster Mini Tacos with Fennel Slaw

Makes 16 tacos

Spicy pimento cheese holds together salty and crispy oysters with a crunchy slaw. It just takes a little fold to bring it all together. Mini tortillas are labeled as "street tacos" by some brands. Most brands of refrigerated oysters have 9 to 12 oysters per 8-ounce container. Open the containers one by one in case you already have 32 oysters from just 3 containers. Then you can save the fourth for another use.

FOR THE CORNMEAL CRUSTED FRIED OYSTERS:

1 cup yellow cornmeal
½ cup all-purpose flour
3 tablespoons cornstarch
1½ teaspoons salt
½ teaspoon freshly ground pepper
4 (8-ounce) containers fresh oysters, well drained
Canola oil, for frying

Whisk together the cornmeal, flour, cornstarch, salt, and pepper.

In a large, heavy Dutch oven, heat 1 inch of canola oil over medium-high heat to 350°F. Set a wire rack over a sheet pan.

Working in batches of about 8 oysters at a time, dredge each oyster in the cornmeal mixture. Carefully place the oysters in the hot oil. Fry, turning often, for about 2 minutes or until golden brown. Drain on the wire rack. Repeat with remaining oysters. Serve, alone or in mini tacos, immediately.

FOR THE FENNEL SLAW:

Makes about 5½ cups

1 large bulb fennel, thinly sliced
½ Vidalia onion, thinly sliced
2 tablespoons mayonnaise
2 tablespoons fresh lime juice
¼ cup chopped fresh cilantro
1 teaspoon red wine vinegar
⅛ teaspoon salt
⅛ teaspoon freshly ground pepper

Combine all ingredients. Chill until ready to serve.

FOR THE MINI TACOS:

16 mini corn tortillas (4 to 5 inches across)
1½ cups Chipotle Pimento Cheese (page 40)
32 Cornmeal Crusted Fried Oysters
4 cups Fennel Slaw
Lime wedges, for serving
Hot sauce, for serving

Heat the tortillas according to package directions. Spread each tortilla with 1½ tablespoons pimento cheese, top with 2 fried oysters and about ¼ cup slaw, and fold. Serve the tacos with lime wedges and hot sauce.

Pimento Cheese Grits

Makes 5½ cups

The key to good grits is cooking time. Stone-ground grits need patience and lots of stirring. My favorite tool to keep grits moving is a fish spatula. The only way to tell if grits are done is by tasting for texture. You shouldn't have to chew. Always wait to add any cheese to grits until they are completely done.

1 cup uncooked stone-ground grits
2 cups whole milk
4 cups water
½ teaspoon salt
1 cup shredded extra-sharp cheddar cheese
4 ounces cream cheese, softened
1 (7-ounce) jar diced pimentos, drained
⅛ teaspoon cayenne pepper

Combine the grits, milk, water, and salt in a large stockpot. Bring to a boil, reduce the heat, and simmer, stirring often, for 1 hour 20 minutes or until the grits are not crunchy when tasted.

Remove from the heat. Stir in the cheddar, cream cheese, pimentos, and cayenne pepper. Continue to stir until the cheeses are melted and completely incorporated. Serve hot.

Pimento Cheese Loaded Nachos

Serves 8 (makes 3¼ cups sauce)

Whether for hosting friends or indulging alone, nachos are loved by everyone. The more toppings, the better. It's the most fun way to clean out the fridge. The divine pimento cheese sauce can double as a hot queso dip.

4 ounces sharp white cheddar cheese
1 (8-ounce) block medium cheddar cheese
2 tablespoons unsalted butter
2 tablespoons all-purpose flour
½ cup half-and-half
1 cup whole milk
⅛ teaspoon ancho chili powder
⅛ teaspoon celery salt
½ teaspoon salt
1 (4-ounce) jar diced pimentos, undrained
Tortilla chips
Toppings: grilled chicken, black beans, pico de gallo, green onions, cilantro, pickled jalapeño

To make the pimento cheese sauce, grate the cheddar cheeses on the small holes of a box grater. Set aside.

Melt the butter in a heavy saucepan over low heat. Whisk in the flour until smooth and cook for 1 minute, whisking constantly. Gradually whisk in the half-and-half, milk, chili powder, celery salt, and salt. Cook over medium heat, whisking constantly, for 2 minutes or until just starting to thicken.

Reduce the heat to low. Stir in the undrained pimentos and the cheeses. Stir until the cheeses are completely melted and smooth. This may take several minutes. Add more half-and-half if the sauce becomes too thick. Keep warm.

Arrange tortilla chips on a sheet pan. Pour about 2½ cups of the pimento cheese sauce over the tortilla chips. Layer with your chosen toppings. If desired, drizzle the remaining pimento cheese sauce over the toppings. Serve immediately.

Pimento Cheese Stuffed Cornbread

Serves 6

I first started "stuffing" cornbread when I was writing my first book. I now add my favorites into cornbread all the time. Pimento cheese works especially well. You can choose any kind you like. One of my favorites is the No-Mayo Pimento Cheese (page 60). Melted cheese and crispy bread is hard to get wrong. Because cornmeal mix has leavening added, it does have an expiration date. Check the package before using to make sure it will still rise.

- 3 tablespoons canola oil
- 1¾ cups self-rising white cornmeal mix (I use White Lily's Buttermilk mix)
- 1 cup whole milk
- 1 large egg
- 1½ teaspoons finely chopped fresh rosemary
- ¾ cup pimento cheese

Preheat the oven to 425°F.

Pour the oil into a 10-inch cast-iron skillet. Place the skillet in the oven as it preheats.

Place the cornmeal mix in a medium mixing bowl. Combine the milk and egg in a small mixing bowl. Stir into the cornmeal. Carefully remove the heated skillet from the oven and pour about half of the hot oil into the batter. It will sizzle and bubble immediately. Stir to incorporate the oil.

Pour about three-quarters of the batter into the hot skillet. Using a tablespoon or a small scoop, drop pimento cheese over the batter in the skillet. Sprinkle half of the rosemary over the pimento cheese. With a fork, gently swirl the pimento cheese through the batter, but do not completely stir it in. Spoon the remaining batter over the pimento cheese and swirl gently. It will not cover the cheese completely. Sprinkle the remaining rosemary over the top.

Bake for 20 to 23 minutes, or until golden brown.

Pimento Cheese Stuffed Burgers

Makes 6

It's common to see burgers piled high with pimento cheese, but I like to stuff the pimento cheese inside so it's a fun surprise with the first bite. Add a slice of cheese to the top if you want extra gooeyness. Using a high-fat beef is key to a good burger. The less fat, the drier the burger will be.

3 ounces sharp cheddar cheese
1 (2-ounce) jar diced pimentos, drained
1 ounce cream cheese, softened
1 tablespoons mayonnaise
2 pounds ground chuck
½ teaspoon salt
¼ teaspoon freshly ground pepper
6 hamburger buns, toasted
Toppings: green leaf lettuce leaves, sliced tomato, dill pickle chips, sliced red onion

Preheat the grill to 350°F (medium-high heat).

Grate the cheddar on the large holes of a box grater. Place the cheddar, pimentos, cream cheese, and mayonnaise in a small bowl. Stir to combine. Divide the ground chuck into six equal portions. Shape each portion into a ball.

Poke a large hole in the center of each ball. Fill with 2 tablespoons pimento cheese and mold the meat to completely enclose it. Flatten the balls to ¾-inch-thick patties, being careful not to open the cheese-stuffed pockets. Sprinkle with salt and pepper.

Grill, with the grill lid closed, for 6 minutes on each side or until the beef is no longer pink. Let stand for 5 minutes. Serve the burgers on the toasted buns with lettuce, tomato, pickles, and onion.

Pimento Cheese Twirls

Makes 16

Look for puff pastry in the freezer case of the grocery store. Make sure you've set aside a little extra time for the sheet of pastry to thaw before unfolding. Any pimento cheese will work for this recipe. Let the pimento cheese come to room temperature for a few minutes for the most spreadability. You can make this recipe your own by adding just about anything extra before rolling into a log. Crumbled bacon, different herbs, and diced fresh jalapeños are all fun additions.

½ (17.3-ounce) package puff pastry
1 cup pimento cheese
2 tablespoons chopped fresh cilantro

Thaw the puff pastry sheet according to package directions. Preheat the oven to 425°F.

On a lightly floured surface, roll the puff pastry into a 12-by-10-inch rectangle. Spread pimento cheese on the pastry, leaving a ½-inch border around the edge.

Sprinkle cilantro over the pimento cheese. Starting with the longer edge of the rectangle, roll the pastry to create a log, as you would for cinnamon rolls.

Chill the log for 40 minutes. Using a sharp knife, slice the log into ¾-inch slices. Arrange on a parchment-lined sheet pan.

Bake at 425°F for 22 minutes. Some cheese will ooze from the twirls and become very crispy. If necessary, snap off the lacy, browned bits when removing the twirls from the pan. (They make yummy snacks for the cook.) Serve the twirls warm or at room temperature.

Savannah Pimento Cheese Pâté

Makes 8 appetizer servings

When sherry and curry powder come together in a recipe, I always think of the old spiral-bound cookbooks from the Lowcountry. Cheese pâté has been around the South for a long time. Making it with a base of pimento cheese makes it even more special.

Patting pimentos dry after draining helps to keep the texture of pimento cheese at its creamiest. It only takes a couple of paper towels to get the job done. I like to serve this pâté on a square platter, but if you like round, shape it into a 6-inch disk.

8 ounces extra-sharp cheddar cheese
8 ounces cream cheese, softened
1 (4-ounce) jar diced pimentos, drained and patted dry
3 tablespoons dry sherry
1 teaspoon curry powder
Pinch of cayenne pepper
¾ cup mango chutney
2 green onions, thinly sliced
Crackers

Grate the cheddar cheese using the large holes of a box grater. Place the cheddar, cream cheese, pimentos, sherry, curry powder, and cayenne pepper in a medium mixing bowl. Stir to combine. On a square platter, shape the pâté into a 1-inch-thick square about 6 inches on a side. Cover and chill for 2 hours.

Before serving, pour mango chutney over the pimento cheese, making sure to cover the entire square. Top with green onions. Serve with crackers.

Store in the refrigerator in an airtight container for up to 3 days.

Pimento Cheese Wafers

Makes about 32

Come over to my house on any day and you're likely to find dough for these in my freezer. They are the perfect snack to slice and pop in the oven right before guests arrive. The logs of dough freeze well for up to a month.

½ cup unsalted butter, softened
1 (8-ounce) block medium cheddar cheese, finely shredded
1 (4-ounce) jar diced pimentos, drained and patted dry
¼ teaspoon salt
⅛ teaspoon cayenne pepper
1½ cups all-purpose flour
Coarsely ground black pepper

Combine the butter, cheddar, pimentos, salt, cayenne pepper, and flour in the bowl of a food processor fitted with the metal blade. Process until the mixture forms a dough.

Shape the dough into a log about 12 inches long. Wrap in plastic wrap and chill for 3 to 24 hours.

Preheat the oven to 375°F.

Cut the log into ⅓-inch-thick slices. Place half the slices on a parchment-lined sheet pan, 2 inches apart. Sprinkle lightly with black pepper. Bake 25 to 28 minutes or until browned. Cool on the pan for 5 minutes, then transfer to a wire rack to cool completely. Repeat with the remaining slices.

Secret Pimento Cheese Deviled Eggs

Makes 24

I collect deviled egg plates pretty much the way that I collect cast iron skillets. They usually have a long history and were important to someone's grandmother at some point in time. I'm always happy to have them come to live with me. The key to the creamiest filling for deviled eggs is grating the yolks instead of using a food processor or fork. Instead of stirring pimento cheese into the yolk mixture as many people do, I like to hide it under the creamy center for a cheesy surprise.

You can choose any pimento cheese you prefer. I like to use the Hoop Pimento Cheese (page 47).

12 large eggs
½ cup mayonnaise
1 teaspoon Dijon mustard
⅛ teaspoon salt
Dash of freshly ground pepper
½ cup pimento cheese
12 bread-and-butter pickles

Cover the eggs with about an inch of cold water in a large saucepan. Bring the water to a boil over high heat. When the water boils, turn the heat off and let the eggs sit for 10 minutes. Submerge the eggs in cold water. Peel the eggs while holding them under running cold water. Slice each egg in half lengthwise.

Remove the yolks from the eggs and place them in a medium mixing bowl. Use a fine grater, such as a Microplane, to grate the yolks. Stir in the mayonnaise, Dijon mustard, salt, and pepper.

Place about 1 teaspoon of pimento cheese in the hollow of each egg half. Using a pastry tip and a ziplock bag, pipe the egg filling on top, concealing the pimento cheese.

Cut the pickles in half (or quarters, if large) and place one piece on the filling of each egg.

Shrimp and Pimento Cheese Crostini

Makes 30

This was one of the first recipes I would make with students, back when I began teaching cooking classes. Students loved them as a heavy appetizer to start the class. I would use the extra-thin white bread from Pepperidge Farm and cut out circles with a two-inch biscuit cutter. After brushing them with melted butter, I'd toast them in the oven to serve as my crostini. They were so very decadent, but time consuming. The easier choice is buying ready-made crostini.

1 (8-ounce) block sharp cheddar cheese
1 (4-ounce) jar diced pimento, drained
¼ cup mayonnaise
½ teaspoon Worcestershire sauce
Pinch of freshly ground pepper
30 crostini
1 pound cooked shrimp (26–32 count), tails removed
Smoked paprika, for garnish

Grate the cheddar using the large holes of a box grater. Place the cheddar, pimento, mayonnaise, Worcestershire, and pepper in a medium mixing bowl. Stir to combine.

Spread about 1 tablespoon of pimento cheese onto each of the crostini. Top with one cooked shrimp. Garnish with a sprinkle of paprika.

Southern Sushi with Pimento Cheese

Makes about 40

I published a version of this recipe in my first cookbook with a less snappy title. It's been one of my most requested recipes for twenty years. My dear friend Virginia Willis brilliantly nicknamed these popular wheels Southern Sushi. I even served them at the James Beard House in New York to oohs and aahs. They can be made days in advance and kept in the fridge until ready to serve.

- 4 ounces cream cheese, softened
- 4 ounces extra-sharp cheddar, finely grated
- 2 tablespoons diced pimentos, drained and patted dry, finely chopped
- 2 tablespoons chopped fresh chives
- 1 (16-ounce) jar pickled okra, drained (about 18 okra pods)
- ⅓ pound thinly sliced Virginia ham (about 8 slices)

Place the cream cheese, cheddar, pimentos, and chives in a medium mixing bowl. Stir to combine.

Trim both ends off each okra pod. On a large cutting board or work surface, lay out the slices of ham. Carefully—trying not to tear the ham—spread about 2 tablespoons of the pimento cheese on each slice, leaving a ¼-inch border.

On the long side of each ham slice, lay 2 or 3 okra pods over the pimento cheese so that they reach from end to end. Roll the ham over the okra. Cover and chill the ham rolls for 3 hours.

Slice the rolls into 1-inch-long segments before serving.

Vidalias Stuffed with Sausage and Pimento Cheese

Makes 4 main-dish or 8 side-dish servings

The low-pH soil around Vidalia, Georgia, is nothing short of a miracle. It's how Vidalia onions have such a mild, sweet flavor. Stuffing them in the same fashion as you would a bell pepper is irresistible. Serve a whole onion as a main dish or cut in half to serve as a side. Depending on the exact size of your onions, you may have a little stuffing left over. Spread it on toast for a quick and hearty breakfast.

- 4 Vidalia onions, about 12 ounces each
- ¼ teaspoon salt
- ⅛ teaspoon freshly ground pepper
- 1 pound ground pork sausage
- 6 ounces sharp cheddar cheese, finely grated
- ¼ cup mayonnaise
- 3 tablespoons diced pimentos, drained
- 1 teaspoon Dijon mustard
- Chopped chives, for garnish

Preheat the oven to 350°F.

Slice ½ inch off the top of each onion. Leaving the root end intact, cut off a small amount of root to make a flat bottom, so the onion will sit upright. Using a grapefruit knife or paring knife, hollow out the center of each onion, leaving a ¾-inch thickness on the bottom and sides. Reserve the centers of the onions for another use.

Sprinkle the onion cavities with the salt and pepper. Arrange the onions in an 8-inch-square baking dish, cover with aluminum foil, and bake at 350°F for 65 minutes or until fork tender. If water has pooled in the onion cavities, carefully spoon it out.

Preheat the broiler with the oven rack positioned 8 inches from the heat. Brown the sausage in a medium skillet over medium heat, stirring often, for 8 minutes or until the meat crumbles and is no longer pink. Drain on paper towels and blot with additional paper towels. Allow to cool.

Combine the sausage, cheddar, mayonnaise, pimentos, and Dijon mustard. Carefully spoon the mixture into the cavities of the hot onions, mounding it. Broil for 2 to 3 minutes or until the stuffing is browned and bubbly. Garnish with chopped chives.

And now, to round out our roster of suggestions, a handful of short takes.

Cheese Straws Topped with Pimento Cheese

Whether homemade or store bought, cheese straws make a super fun base for a little mound of pimento cheese. Any version will do, but I especially like to use the Pimento Cheese, Augusta National Style (page 69). After piling pimento cheese onto the flat side of the cheese straw, sprinkle with finely chopped toasted pecans. Chill for 2 hours before serving.

Spicy Pimento Cheese Dog

My sister's husband, Tom, makes a mean pimento cheese hot dog. For his sky-high version, top a grilled 100 percent beef hot dog with Pickled Jalapeño Pimento Cheese (page 66), your favorite coleslaw, spicy pickle relish, yellow mustard, a little ketchup, and hot sauce. It's not complete without a good cold beer.

Pimento Cheese Toast with Fried Egg

A favorite breakfast of mine is made with a good slice of locally baked bread that's been toasted just until it's slightly crispy and spread with pimento cheese. I like to top it with a fried egg right out of the skillet so it slightly melts the pimento cheese.

Pimento Cheese Bites

For a quick appetizer, top store-bought crostini with pimento cheese and broil just until the cheese begins to bubble. Top with crumbled bacon before serving.

Pimento Cheese Fries

I keep all-natural frozen French fries in my freezer all the time. After baking fries according to the manufacturer's directions, push the fries together slightly on the sheet pan. Preheat the broiler. Spoon dollops of pimento cheese over the fries. Broil 5 inches from the heat for about 3 minutes or until the cheese is melted. Serve immediately.

Pimento Cheese Tartlets

If there's one item in the freezer case of the grocery store that is the greatest gift to entertaining, it's phyllo shells. Fill shells with pimento cheese, add about a teaspoon of pepper jelly, and bake at 350°F for 10 minutes. Top with chopped fresh chives before serving.

Love at First Taste

We did not grow up eating pimento cheese. My childhood memories of cheese are of macaroni and cheese, grilled cheese sandwiches, and summer evenings sitting on the front porch with my grandfather eating hoop cheese, bologna, and saltine crackers. I had my first taste of pimento cheese when I moved to Georgia almost twenty years ago. I was teaching garde-manger at a local culinary school and, through studying the history of cheese, discovered this Southern staple. It was love at first taste. Through the years I've tasted many different versions of pimento cheese and decided to make one that spoke to my family roots. My recipe is a mix of cheeses, smoked bacon, and smoked paprika. I add these ingredients to an egg salad filling and serve it as a deviled egg. Although I didn't grow up eating pimento cheese, this recipe makes me think of home.

Jennifer Hill Booker

Author and food advocate
Atlanta, Georgia

Acknowledgments

We all have a common conversation point of food, and for me lately it's been much more about pimento cheese than anything else. This book has developed in a way that no other has in my career. Once others learned I was working on a pimento cheese project, they tended to tell me their stories of pimento cheese and why they love it so. It has been a magical journey.

Neighborhood friends went over the top with all things pimento cheese. Ba Steedman talked me through her mother's "cheese pimento" and even drove down the hill to my house, spoon in hand, to taste to see if my version was close. Hint: it wasn't, not that time, but we got there. Theresa Hunnicutt's pimento cheese came up in conversation at church, and she came the few blocks over to my house with her sample in hand. Virginia Stutsman is another neighbor, and a staple employee at my daughter's school, who shared the beginnings of her crazy-cool pimento cheese history in the concession stand at a soccer game. Virginia mentioned that her family had a unique history with pimento cheese. She shared with me the story of how her grandparents created the pimento cheese legacy at the Masters and even Bobby Jones was a fan.

I am deeply grateful for the authors who shared their pimento cheese stories and love of the spread that rules the South. Carrie Morey, Anne Byrn, Jennifer Booker, and Jessica Little were beyond gracious with me. I've written about Crystal Leach in several books. She makes the world's best pepper jelly. Pepper jelly and pimento cheese will always go together, and I just hope my recipes do her jelly justice. Kelly Sanders bounced pimento cheese ideas around with me and is a food friend I cherish dearly.

Shelley Renner and Sherry Sheppard shared why they love pineapple in pimento cheese, and they successfully converted me to their side. It's now one of my favorite combinations. When I buy local pimento cheese, it's Lindsey Payne's. She makes pimento-less cheese and it's incredible! She graciously shared her recipe for this book. I was struggling with pimento cheese biscuits and turned to Cynthia Graubart and Virginia Willis for help. They should run a hotline for frustrated cooks. Ivy Odom pulled out her phone and connected me with one of the makers of my favorite Southern cheese, Sweet Grass Dairy.

This is my ninth book, and my career in food writing would never have happened without Nathalie Dupree. There's never been a book I've written without her influence or advice. I will love her as long as I'm alive.

My parents, Mandy and William Dopson, ate just as much pimento cheese as I did during the writing of this book. I'm pretty sure they enjoyed every single second of it. I am grateful for each stepping-stone they provided for me growing up so I can do what I do.

I wish I knew how many times the subject of pimento cheese came up in conversations with my friends at UGA Press over the last several years. I'm grateful for their patience and their hard work to make such an unforgettable book. Nate Holly, Erin Kirk, Lisa Bayer, Anna Forrester, Elizabeth Crowley, Elizabeth Adams, and Ann Marlowe were easy to work with and played a role in making this collection one worthy of every single cheesy slather.

The talents of photographer Kathryn McCrary, food stylist Ali Ramee, and prop stylist Missie Crawford came together to create an absolute dream team of pimento cheese glory. They made sure every single spreader and ooey gooey cheesy bite was literally irresistible.

Kevin, Camden, and Adair are used to being told that it's pimento cheese for supper (again) and accept a cheese-laden menu with a smile. Camden and Adair are sweet helpers with book signings and cooking demos and all of the schlepping that those entail. If Kevin has carried one box of books, he's carried ten thousand. He has always lovingly supported my writing and my cooking. These three people are my home.

Bibliography

Adams, Natalie P., J. W. Joseph, and Denise P. Messick. "Tilling the Earth." Georgia Department of Natural Resources, Historic Preservation Division, October 1, 2001.

Bull, Andy. "The Man Who Captured the Unique Flavour of Augusta." *Guardian*, April 6, 2016. https://www.theguardian.com/sport/blog/2016/apr/06/the-masters-golf-augusta-pimento-cheese-sandwich-nick-rangos-2016.

Byrn, Anne. "Cheese, Peppers and Possibilities: Anne Byrn on the History of Pimento Cheese in the South." *Southern Kitchen*, September 17, 2021. https://www.southernkitchen.com/story/lifestyle/2021/07/22/anne-byrns-history-pimento-cheese-south/8063150002.

Culinary Depot. "What Is a Pimento? Origins, Recipes, And More!" February 9, 2023. https://www.culinarydepotinc.com/blog/what-is-a-pimento-origins-recipes-and-more.

Easters, Melita. "Inspired by Rosalynn Carter's Airplane Pimento Cheese Sandwiches? Try Our Recipe!" *Georgia Win List*, December 1, 2023. https://www.gawinlist.com/inspired-by-rosalynn-carters-airplane-pimento-cheese-sandwiches-try-our-recipe.

Fater, Luke. "The Sandwich Scandal at the Heart of the World's Greatest Golfing Event." *Atlas Obscura*, April 9, 2021. https://www.atlasobscura.com/articles/masters-pimento-cheese-sandwich.

Fery, Richard L., and Judy A. Thies. "'Truhart-NR,' A Root-Knot Nematode-Resistant, Pimento-Type Pepper." *American Society for Horticultural Science* 46.5 (May 2011).

Georgia Department of Agriculture. *Agricultural Heritage of Georgia*. N.d.

Georgia Historical Society. "Georgia Experiment Station." https://www.georgiahistory.com/ghmi_marker_updated/georgia-experiment-station.

Greenlee, Cynthia R. "Pimento-cracy," *Oxford American*, March 23, 2021. https://oxfordamerican.org/magazine/issue-112-spring-2021/pimento-cracy.

———. "Reinventing the Peach, the Pimento, and Regional Identity." *Issues in Science and Technology*, Summer 2022.

Herbst, Ron, and Sharon Tyler. *The New Food Lover's Companion* 4th ed. Hauppauge, N.Y.: Barron's Educational Services, 2007.

Hill, Kathleen Thompson. "Really Grate: The Kathleen Thompson Hill Collection of Cheese Graters." The Cheese Professor, March 17, 2021. https://www.cheeseprofessor.com/blog/antique-cheese-graters.

Kovalchick, Kara. "What Are Pimentos, and How Do They Get Inside Olives?" *Mental Floss*, April 1, 2023. https://www.mentalfloss.com/article/54749/what-are-pimentos-and-how-do-they-get-inside-olives.

Levin, Joe. "How the Master's Made Pimento Cheese Southern." The Word from Religion of Sports, April 12, 2024. https://religionofsports.substack.com/p/how-the-masters-made-pimento-cheese?utm_source=substack&utm_medium=email&utm_content=share.

McNally, Frank. "Tracking Masters Food Prices as Far Back as We Can." The Great Golf Blog, March 2020. https://www.thegreatgolfblog.com/blog/tracking-masters-food-prices-as-far-back-as-we-can.

Mirshak, Meg. "Augusta Family Prepared Sandwiches in Early Days of Masters Tournament." *Augusta Chronicle*, April 9, 2014. https://www.augusta.com/masters/story/news/augusta-family-prepared-sandwiches-early-days-masters-tournament.

Moss, Robert. "Creating a (New) Southern Icon: The Curious History of Pimento Cheese." RobertFMoss.com, February 21, 2011. https://www.robertfmoss.com/features/Creating-a-New-Southern-Icon-the-Curious-History-of-Pimento-Cheese.

———. "From Scientific Cuisine to Southern Icon: The Real History of Pimento Cheese." *Serious Eats*, August 10, 2018. https://www.seriouseats.com/history-southern-food-pimento-cheese.

Reese, Nicholas. "Pass the Mayo: The Story of the South's Legendary Spread." *New Orleans Historical*, November 9, 2019. https://neworleanshistorical.org/items/show/1424.

Slack, Susan Fuller. "Pimento Cheese: A Bowlful of Southern Comfort." *Columbia Metropolitan*, September 2017. https://columbiametro.com/article/pimento-cheese.

Stevens, Ashlie. "The History of Durkee Famous Sauce, a Forgotten Vintage Luxury with Modern Condiment Shelf Appeal." *Salon*, April 11, 2021. https://www.salon.com/2021/04/11/the-history-of-durkee-famous-sauce-a-forgotten-vintage-luxury-with-modern-condiment-shelf-appeal.

Thompson, Wright. "A Sandwich Stumper at the Masters." ESPN, April 11, 2013. https://www.espn.com/golf/masters13/story/_/id/9159515/golf-sandwich-stumper-masters.

Upstate Business Journal. "The Duke's Century." June 8, 2017. https://upstatebusinessjournal.com/economic-development/the-dukes-century/#:~:text=As%20legend%20has%20it%2C%20on,earning%20two%20cents%20per%20sandwich.

Wallace, Emily Elizabeth. "It Was There for Work: Pimento Cheese in the Carolina Piedmont." Master's thesis, University of North Carolina at Chapel Hill, 2010.

Index

Page numbers in italics refer to recipes.

About the Author

Rebecca Lang is a ninth-generation Southerner and the author of *Pimento Cheese* and *Y'all Come Over* as well as seven other cookbooks. She has worked on the editorial aspect of more than thirty books. She has appeared on the Food Network as a judge for *Chopped Junior*, cooked at the James Beard House, and been featured in more than fifty nationally televised *Southern Living* food segments as well as cooked on *Fox & Friends Weekend*. Rebecca has been featured in the *Wall Street Journal*, *Parade* magazine, *Martha Stewart Living*, *Simply Recipes*, the *Los Angeles Times*, the *Atlanta Journal-Constitution*, the *Washington Post*, *Glamour*, and *Fitness* magazine.

Rebecca is one of the few cookbook authors ever to sell out of books on QVC. She was named as a finalist for Georgia Author of the Year. She is a proud graduate of the University of Georgia as well as Johnson & Wales University. She serves on the board of One Hundred Miles and on the UGA Press Advisory Board. She lives with her husband, Kevin, two children, Camden and Adair, and a Cavalier King Charles in Athens, Georgia.